the way of mary

Praying and Living Her Words

KRISTEN JOHNSON INGRAM, O.S.A.

Liguori
ONE LIGUORI DRIVE
LIGUORI MO 63057-9999
314.464.2500

Imprimi Potest:
Richard Thibodeau, C.SS.R.
Provincial, Denver Province
The Redemptorists

Imprimatur:
+ Paul A. Zipfel, V.G.
Auxiliary Bishop, Archdiocese of St. Louis

ISBN 0-7648-0033-7
Library of Congress Catalog Card Number: 96-78940

Copyright © 1997, Kristen Johnson Ingram
Printed in the United States of America
97 98 99 00 01 5 4 3 2 1

Scripture quotations are from the *New Revised Standard Version of the Bible*, copyright © 1989 by the Division of Christian Education of the National Council of the Churches of Christ in the USA. Used with permission. All rights reserved.

Cover design by Christine Kraus

For Susan:
Blessed is she who believes.

CONTENTS

how to use this book

They welcomed the message very eagerly and examined the scriptures every day to see whether these things were so.

Acts 17:11

∽

Dear Mary,
pray for me as I seek to be
what you are. Amen

This is a book about the *biblical* Mary, written for all who want a deeper relationship with Christ. Based on the gospel accounts of Mary's life and speech, it invites you to explore the words of Mary and bring their meaning into the contemporary moment. There are many ways to approach Mary. The Mary of history, the Mary of theology, the Mary of Christian tradition, and the Mary of the Bible all contribute to an understanding of the woman who became the Mother of God and who was Christ's first disciple. This book focuses on the biblical Mary, on her words and actions as presented by New Testament writers. It offers you an opportunity to make Mary's brief words into six prayers and a rule of life.

How you will use this book depends on who you are. If you're a man or woman reading for inspiration, you can simply pick up this volume and go straight through it. Keep your Bible nearby as you read this book, and, if possible, check the verses in each chapter in some other translations, such as the *Revised English Bible* and the *New American Bible*, for other interpretations of the gospel stories about Mary. Use your journal to follow the ideas presented at the end of each chapter in the section called "Living Her Words." (You don't need a fancy leather-bound book; a spiral notebook that you can keep in a private place is fine.) This activity is an important part of *The Way of Mary*. Through reflecting on each chapter and trying out the suggested prayers or writing, you actually participate in the book itself.

At the very end of each chapter, you'll find a section titled "Reflections." Use these questions to look inside yourself for new ways that God is acting to make you more like Mary.

If you're a group facilitator or RCIA instructor, you'll probably want to consult the Leader's Guide at the end of the book. That guide will help also if you're planning a retreat. You might want to get a copy of the book for each retreatant so you can all use the exercises at the end of each chapter. Use the reflections for each chapter as a springboard for either prayer or discussion.

If you're the pastor of your church and you want to preach a homily series about Mary, you can condense the material into your own words and include some material from the exercises in "Living Her Words."

However you use it, I hope you'll discover new facets of our Lady's personality by doing as the early converts did when they "examined the scriptures every day to see whether these things were so" (Acts 17:11).

This book grew out of a homily I preached in my church several years ago for the Feast of the Annunciation. I didn't include either apocrypha about Mary or the many messages reported at her appearances at such sites as Lourdes, Fatima, and Medjugorje. I wanted to find the Mary of *Scripture*—and to see what inspiration I could find there. I found a new way of prayer, and it is my privilege to share it with you.

CHAPTER ONE

the virgin mary

What the Bible Record Shows

Let your adornment be the inner self with the lasting beauty of a
gentle and quiet spirit, which is very precious in God's sight.

1 Peter 3:4

O God,
grant that I may find meaning
in the words of the Blessed Virgin
as they are recorded in Scripture;
and I beseech you to send the Holy Spirit
to guide me in my search. Amen

I was standing with a tour group in Jerusalem's Church of the Holy Sepulcher when I saw a woman slip a ring, set with an immense diamond, onto the outstretched wooden hand of a statue of the Sorrowful Mother. The ring was probably worth a fortune. Through the tears that streamed down her face, the woman smiled and kissed the fingertips of the statue.

A passerby might have thought that the woman was deranged or maybe even idolatrous. Actually, she was neither. She was donating to the work of the Fathers at the great shrine of Christianity. She was also expressing her love—one person's reflection of a universal love—for the woman whom the Catholic tradition calls Mother of God and whom the Orthodox tradition calls *Theotokos* or God-bearer.

Only Christ himself activates more human love than Mary. Devout Christians have loved our Lord's mother from the earliest days of the Church, and few prayers are said more frequently worldwide than the Hail Mary of the rosary. With each of her appearances—Guadalupe, Banneaux, Lourdes, Cracow, Fatima, and Medjugorje—love for the Virgin grew by leaps and bounds. Saints like Bernadette have heard her voice and reported her words.

When we seek the life of the Blessed Virgin Mary in the Bible, it's hard to find many of her actual speeches. But Mary was part of the central act of history. By giving birth to Jesus she participated in our salvation, and so we long to hear her voice. She was a quiet woman, a woman who kept her own counsel and pondered things in her heart, but surely she spoke more than we find in the four Bible incidents.

Why does Scripture record so few of her words? Perhaps God chose to reveal only a few of Mary's words to us through Scripture so that we would seek her in other ways; or perhaps the gospel writers—charged with zeal in telling the Good News of Jesus Christ—just didn't record much of what she said.

Did Mary speak of the future as she lay on the straw of the stable, giving birth to the Savior of the world? When Wise Men followed the star to worship and bring gifts, did she express joy or confusion? Shepherds came and angels sang, but we only know that she "treasured all these words and pondered them in her heart" (Luke 2:19). We don't know what she said to them.

In the Temple Simeon told Mary that he had seen the Savior and that a sword would pierce her own soul, but we have no recorded answer to those terrifying words. And though we can visit a tiny, ancient Coptic church in Cairo, Egypt, on the site of a house where the Holy Family is said to have sojourned in their flight from Herod, we can only guess at what she said or did while they lived there. Did she make friends among the women who pounded their clothes at the edge of the Nile? Or did she keep to herself, hiding her child from the whole world?

Legends abound, but the Bible doesn't say.

When Joseph moved the family back to the poor village of Nazareth, was she glad or sorry to go? Did she leave friends in Egypt? How did she and Jesus relate during his adolescence and early twenties? We wonder if Joseph died early in the life of Jesus or lived until close to the end of his ministry.

And when Mary stood at the foot of the cross, listening to her dying son present her to John, how did she respond? The Bible says she went to live with the beloved disciple "from that hour" (John 19:27), but the writer does not record her words to him. We don't even know what she said at the tomb!

However, Mary *did* leave us a few words—words that translate into six prayers for us and a perfect rule of life.

The Bible record of Mary actually begins not in the New Testament, but in the Hebrew Scriptures, with the Creation story. Eve, whose name means *life,* was the symbol of female creation. Even though she had been brought to life by the breath of God, placed in companionship with the first man, and given a home in Paradise, Eve failed to sustain her faith in God's beneficence. Despite being the first woman to *see* God face to face, Eve's restlessness and gullibility led her to yield to the serpent's temptations. Through her, Earth lost its innocence.

In Adam and Eve all people died. But despite Eve's fatal sin in eating and in giving her husband the fruit, she still had God's breath within her. Her descendant, Mary of Nazareth, gave birth to Jesus, the Christ who atoned for human sin.

The Bible scenes of Mary begin with the archangel Gabriel, sent from heaven to salute her and to tell her that she will give birth to the Messiah. The young virgin asks, *"How can this be?"* (Luke 1:34). She has no husband, has never been with a man. But when Gabriel explains, she responds, *"Let it be with me according to your word"* (Luke 1:38).

Mary then hurries to the hill country to see her cousin Elizabeth, a heretofore barren woman who has also conceived miraculously. When Elizabeth hears Mary's greeting, her unborn child—who will one day be called John the Baptist—leaps in her womb. Elizabeth cries out in words of praise, and Mary responds with the Magnificat, *"My soul magnifies the Lord"* (Luke 1:46).

What the Bible Record Shows   3

The next time we hear Mary speak, Jesus is twelve years old. Mary has been looking for him for three agonizing days. When she finds him in the Temple talking to the teachers, she reacts in a gentle but very human way: *"Child, why have you treated us like this? Look, your father and I have been searching for you in great anxiety"* (Luke 2:48). After Jesus tries to reassure her, she takes him home, and he is "obedient to them" (Luke 2:51).

The last of Mary's words are spoken at the wedding in Cana. A young couple has been feasting with their friends and relations, perhaps for several days. When the wine is exhausted, Mary goes to her grown son, who is attending the wedding with his disciples, and she says, *"They have no wine"* (John 2:3). Jesus refuses her request, but she simply turns to the servants and says, *"Do whatever he tells you"* (John 2:5).

The gospel writers mention Mary in another story, a story in which she fears for her son's safety (see Matthew 12:24-50 and Mark 3:22-35). The Pharisees were noising about that Jesus was possessed by Beelzebub, the devil. With some men of the family, she rushes to where Jesus is, and he makes it clear he is not in danger. He then raises each of us to the place of family members by saying, "Whoever does the will of God is my brother and sister and mother" (Mark 3:35).

We see Mary again at the foot of the cross in mute agony as John takes her as his mother (John 29:25-27). Then we find her with the Magdalene at the empty tomb (Matthew 28:1-8). Our Lord's mother is last mentioned by name as she sits with the disciples in the upper room at Pentecost (Acts 1:14–2:11). Both Luke, the author of Acts, and Paul, in his letter to the Romans and his second letter to Timothy, refer to her when they say that Jesus was of the seed of David, for that was Mary's ancestral house. (See Acts 13:22-23; Romans 1:3; 2 Timothy 2:8.)

Although we have prayed *to* Mary for two millennia, asking for her intercessions and favors, we may have forgotten to pray *with* her. But the brief sentences Mary left us can become prayers that still have meaning in human life, even in these high-impact, stress-filled days. Saying Mary's words as they are found in Scripture can bring us closer to Christ, create intimacy with God, and sustain a vital relationship with the Woman whose "Yes!" brought salvation into the world.

Each chapter in this book examines Mary's actual words from the Bible, then offers some ideas about what these words can mean for prayerful men and women in our time.

living her words

1. Scripture Passages

Pick out three events in the Bible record from the following list. Don't just stick to those you're most familiar with. You might want to include two familiar ones—such as the birth of Jesus and his crucifixion—but add a third one you haven't thought so much about. Then follow the directions for meditation and journaling.

Genesis 1:27-28; Genesis 2:18-24; Genesis 3:2-20
The story of Eve and the curse God places on her after she and Adam sin in the Garden of Eden.

Matthew 1:18-25; Matthew 2:1-12
Jesus is conceived by the Holy Spirit, born in Bethlehem, and visited by the Magi.

Luke 1:26-56; Luke 2:1-52
Luke tells the story of Jesus' early life from the Annunciation to the Finding in the Temple.

Matthew 2:13-15,19-23
After an angel warns Joseph of Herod's plot against their child, Mary and Joseph flee to Egypt. When Herod the Great dies, they return and decide to live in Nazareth.

Luke 2:41-50
Mary and Joseph take Jesus to the Temple in Jerusalem. They lose him in the crowd and search three days for their son. They find him back in the Temple, confounding the scholars.

John 2:1-11
Jesus attends a wedding with his disciples, and Mary tells him the host is out of wine.

Mark 3:20-22,31-35; Matthew 12:22-25,46-49
Fearing for Jesus' safety, Mary and his kinsmen come to protect him.

What the Bible Record Shows   5

John 19:25-27
Jesus looks down at Mary from the cross; John takes her to his home.

Acts 1:12-14
Mary is among the disciples who gather before Pentecost.

2. Meditation

After you have read and re-read a Bible passage, spend some time in meditation on the event you've chosen. Place yourself in the scene, and let yourself *see* Mary and her Holy Family. If you're in Bethlehem, are you a shepherd or perhaps a midwife, called in by a pleading Joseph? How does Mary look? Try to hear the animal sounds in the stable—sheep chewing and bleating, birds fluttering down to eat some of the seed from the hay, the soft braying of a donkey—and the sounds of rustling straw and a whimpering baby. Smell the rich barn smell, the golden scent of straw, the darker, muskier odor of animal fur. In your meditation, touch Mary's cloak or sandal, maybe even offer to hold the infant.

Does Mary speak to you? Does she speak to anyone else? Can you hear her prayers? What do you want to say to her?

3. Journal

Write down in a notebook or journal the thoughts and feelings you experienced in your meditation on one event, then meditate on the next event and journal that experience. If you want to continue this kind of reflection, choose *all* of the Bible passages above, meditate on each one, then journal your thoughts, ideas, or feelings. Keep your notebook or journal separate from your day book or other lists.

reflections

How did God speak to me today in the Scriptures?
In what way do I have more life as I read the Bible?
How well do I know Mary as I begin this spiritual journey?

CHAPTER TWO

how can this be?

The Prayer of Awe and Wonder

In the sixth month the angel Gabriel was sent by God to a town in Galilee called Nazareth, to a virgin engaged to a man whose name was Joseph, of the house of David. The virgin's name was Mary. And he came to her and said, "Greetings, favored one! The Lord is with you." But she was much perplexed by his words and pondered what sort of greeting this might be. The angel said to her, "Do not be afraid, Mary, for you have found favor with God. And now, you will conceive in your womb and bear a son, and you will name him Jesus. He will be great, and will be called the Son of the Most High, and the Lord God will give to him the throne of his ancestor David. He will reign over the house of Jacob forever, and of his kingdom there will be no end." Mary said to the angel, "How can this be, since I am a virgin?"

Luke 1:26-34

∞

The scene: Nazareth was a small, poor village in the rocky hills, several miles from the Sea of Galilee. Although the gospels don't give us a setting for Gabriel's visit, ancient tradition says that the angel came to Mary as she was filling her water jar at the village spring. The same spring is still the main source of water in modern Nazareth, and you may drink from it if you visit Israel.

∞

Dear God,
teach me the same awe and wonder
shown by the Blessed Virgin Mary. Amen

Traditions say that Mary was thirteen years old, filling her water jar at Nazareth's town well when Gabriel appeared to her—and that she dropped and broke the vessel when the archangel spoke.

"Greetings, favored one!" Gabriel cried. "The Lord is with you."

No wonder Mary dropped her clay pitcher: the plain people of her small Galilean town certainly didn't greet each other that way. To complicate things, the stranger's words were pretty close to worship! Imagine, then, how much *more* startled she was when she discovered that her visitor was the archangel Gabriel, who went on to reveal that she would give birth to the Savior of the world.

After all, Mary was just a village girl with no education, no money, not even married yet; surely she wondered why God chose her, of all the women in the world.

And the angel said she would—*what*? Bear a child?

"How can this be?" she murmured, uttering the first of the recorded prayers we can say with Mary. "I am a virgin."

Contrast with Zechariah

This moment wasn't the first time the archangel Gabriel had been questioned. Just a few months earlier, Gabriel had visited Zechariah, the husband of Mary's older relative Elizabeth. God apparently didn't need to send an angelic messenger to Elizabeth herself, for when that spiritually mature woman conceived, she immediately gave the credit to God, not needing an angel to tell her this was a miracle!

But Zechariah the priest wasn't so sure of God's hand in this. When Gabriel suddenly appeared in the Temple to say that barren, middle-aged Elizabeth would conceive—and conceive a prophet who would be filled from birth with the Holy Spirit—Zechariah was suspicious. He tried to put God to the test: "How can I be sure of this?" he asked.

Zechariah asked for *proof*—proof that the archangel was telling the truth! He actually wanted to put Gabriel on probation, wanted the angel to give him some sign or certainty, wanted to make him prove that Elizabeth would actually conceive.

Zechariah was struck dumb for his doubt and suspicion.

Contrast Mary's reaction. She also questioned the angel—but she spoke not out of misgiving or distrust, but from *wonder.* How indeed could this happen? In all the history of Israel, had there ever been a virgin birth?

And beyond the question of conception, the angel had announced that Mary's son would be the Messiah—the Son of God! How could *that* be?

Would this Messiah put an end to human rule and bring the divine kingdom to earth? How *could* this be? Mary was astonished by Gabriel's foretelling, overwhelmed by the power of God.

God Honors Wonder

When Mary asked "How can this be?," she was in a state not of suspicion but of awe. God always honors reverent awe and wonder. Prayers of astonishment don't require a *complete* answer, but God will always offer satisfaction to those who pray with such reverence. Within the limits of our understanding, we receive answers to our wonder about the universe, about the mystery of life, about the enigma of relationships.

Scientists who look into the heavens with wonder will slowly unravel the clues God places throughout physical creation, just as you who pray diligently for wisdom receive insight and even revelation.

So when a young girl of Nazareth asked "How can this be?," the archangel Gabriel—who stands always in the presence of God—gave her an answer. He explained that the Holy Spirit would come over her, and the power of the Most High would "overshadow" her, so that her child would be called Son of God. Then Gabriel added that Mary's relative Elizabeth, thought to be barren, was now six months pregnant. "For nothing will be impossible with God."

You can share Mary's awe. At moments, every one of us is overwhelmed by God's action: a friend is miraculously healed; the old, gray-barked dogwood tree suddenly bursts into bloom; an astronomer reveals that he has found a galaxy a hundred billion light years away; a child or grandchild is born. You are always praying, whether you consciously address your prayers to God or not. Sister John Backenstos, OHN—a Holy Name sister who lives and ministers in a mountain parish and who runs a retreat house in the deep woods of Oregon—says, "You can't *not* pray." And any time you feel a sense of astonishment and awe, you have joined the young Virgin of Nazareth in prayer. When you're overwhelmed by that pink dogwood tree or a double rainbow in a stormy sky, when you're astonished and baffled by the Atonement or the complexity of the human brain, whenever you look at God's work and think *How can this be?*, you're praying the words of Mary.

The Awe of Sorrow or Bitterness

Sometimes your awe may be tinged with negatives. Maybe your friend is *not* healed but dies, in spite of your earnest prayers. Or your teenager rebels and starts running with a bad crowd. Or a city endures major disaster from hurricane or earthquake or flood. And since you've tried hard to be a good friend or parent or steward, and since you're a faithful Christian, you ask God, "Why? How can these things be?"

But this time you don't speak out of delight in God's action or creation. You are expressing grief and anger. Then you are not expressing wonder when you ask "How can this be?" You are asking God to explain the world—a world that includes sickness, death, sorrow, and all kinds of trouble.

The explanation is in Scripture. Jesus never promised that Christians would not suffer; he said, "In the world you face persecution" (John 16:33). We don't know why prayers apparently aren't answered the way we want them to be, why hail beats the blossoms off fruit trees, or why children are born with incurable diseases. Saint Paul reminds us that "the whole creation has been groaning" (Romans 8:22) in expectation of redemption, that we were saved *in hope*, not in earthly *fulfillment*. As Christians, when we ask how and why of God, we must ask in the context of hope, trusting "that all things work together for good for those who love God" (Romans 8:28). This way, no matter how difficult the circumstances or how highly charged our feelings, we can still build up the store of holiness within and remain in fellowship with Christ and Mary.

Acedia: When Your Wonder Is Gone

Maybe you've had a hard time: a long string of illnesses; a broken relationship or even a divorce; a business or academic failure. Now you'd *like* to pray the prayer of awe and wonder, but no matter how many sunsets you witness or how often you kneel before the altar, you can't seem to rouse anything within yourself. You feel like a stone. *Pray* the words of Mary? On such a day you may hardly believe she ever said them.

If what you're suffering from is depression, you can get help. If your problem is fairly recent and is the result of a bad time, *give in to it*. Spend a few days lounging around. Take a sick day or two off work and rest. Try to journal your feelings or talk to a good friend or priest who will listen without trying to fix things.

If your depression is longer term, you may need some counseling or medicine or both. Don't hesitate to obtain what you need, because depression is a real illness and should be taken seriously.

On the other hand, if your problem has spiritual components, if your loss of awe and reverence comes after disappointment or a long string of what you consider to be "no" answers to your prayers, you may need a spiritual cure. Christian writers and teachers through the centuries have described this condition as *acedia*—the sin of sloth.

This is the time when prayer would be the cure—but you can't or won't pray. You're bored, dispirited, maybe even faithless. God seems far away. Your prayers, if you can muster any up, are only going to go as high as the ceiling.

You'll need to do three things to regain spiritual health: *confess*, *repent*, and *praise*. Before you're ready to confess, you'll need to spend some time reflecting. Saint Thomas Aquinas said that envy always precedes acedia. During your reflection time, see if the state of sloth you're in began soon after you felt that you couldn't have or do as much as someone else.

If you envy someone else's situation rather than feeling content with what you *do* have, you're setting yourself up for the sloth that comes from envious frustration.

Sacramental reconciliation is the specific cure for the sin of sloth. *Confess*, even if you don't *feel* sorry, because then you can receive forgiveness. And if you can remember the moment of envy that started the process, confess that, too.

Receive your absolution with as much joy as you can, and then *repent*. Repentance doesn't mean to be sorry or feel guilty; it means to *turn around*, to declare a state of opposites. Whatever form your acedia has taken, do just the opposite. If you have been sleeping late, get up early. If you've been thinking only of your own misery, go for a walk and look at creation, send birthday and get-well cards to people, volunteer at a day-care center. You know better than anyone what you need to do to turn things around.

After confession and repentance, you're ready to begin the third part of the cure—*praise*. Start a daily list of things that inspire your awe and make you ask, "How can this be?" Look for beauty outdoors and within yourself, goodness in the face of evil, the love of your friends or even your dog or cat. Then every day, read your list and praise God—aloud, if possible. Soon you'll discover that what you were doing consciously and with effort has become a way of life, a way of praying the words of Mary.

Everyday Excitement

Praying in a state of awe means letting every day bring new excitement into your spiritual life. You may be in unhappy circumstances—but you can't *be* unhappy, if you're expressing a joyful adoration toward God and God's action and works. You may be ill, but your spirit can soar. You may be physically deaf to music and human voices, but inwardly you can hear the heavenly host praising God. No matter how hard your life, there's always room in it for reverence and adoration.

The prayer of awe and wonder is a Sabbath within the hard work of living. You can stop and reflect on whatever makes your heart leap with devotion: an autumn leaf, a baby's toenail, a switch from oppression to democracy in a Third World country, an unexpected act of love from a family member, even a loaf of bread that comes out of the oven. And of course Mary's "How can this be!" is what you can pray when the priest elevates the host at Mass. How, indeed, can it be that God can be human, sacrificed, and resurrected, and the thin wafer of bread somehow become his body?

Seek the joy of wonder. If you love nature, take a few minutes every day to *look*, whether at the patterns frost makes on your windows or the shadows a maple tree casts on the lawn; walk, if you can, and see how many times in a mile you can be moved with awe.

If your life includes caring for small children, enjoy their laughter and marvel at their beauty. As you wash the ice cream from their faces, notice how differently every little mouth is formed, how individual each nose and chin. If the children you care for are ill or mentally challenged, praise God for each tiny healing or progress.

The psalmist says to the Lord: "You are holy, enthroned on the praises of Israel" (Psalm 22:3). This doesn't mean that God depends on our praise. It means that when you glorify God, you're entering God's dwelling place of glory. Praise isn't the same as thanks. My husband may say "Thank you for the good dinner," and I'm happy to hear it; but his *praise*—"Kris, you're a wonderful woman!"—makes me feel very warm toward him.

And if you can't find three things a day to praise God for, three things a day about which to say, "How can this be?" in a state of wonder, pray for God to open your eyes and ears and to deliver you from stoniness of heart. The more you seek what the Jewish theologian Martin Buber called "radical amazement," the closer you'll feel toward God and the more fellowship in prayer you will share with the whole Church—including our Lord's mother.

living her words

1. Look at Mary

You can find a number of great paintings of the Annunciation, usually showing Mary in a beautiful bower or a marble balcony, richly dressed, sometimes reading a book. But how do *you* visualize the scene? Is Mary beautifully gowned, blond and serene—or is she a sun-browned peasant girl carrying a water jar? Is the sun shining, or is a March wind whipping her cloak?

Imagine that you are present, perhaps as Mary's friend or a cousin (not Elizabeth), or as an unknown observer. What emotions do you see in Mary's face when Gabriel appears? And when she asks How can this be?, what do you hear in her voice? Is she poised and sure of herself? Confused and shy? After Gabriel leaves, does she speak to you?

2. Look at Yourself

How many times in a day do you encounter awe or wonder? For a whole week, keep track of the wonders about you and the wonder you feel. Pray with Mary, "How can this be?" each time you find yourself amazed or awed. Journal the experiences and thank God for each time this happens to you.

3. Make an Offering

Make a small offering to God for your awe. Next time you see or hear or understand something that makes your heart leap, journal it (as in number 2 above), and then burn a stick of incense, press a tiny flower in your Bible, sing a hymn, or cook a special meal for your family, as thanksgiving for your sense of wonder.

reflections

Did I allow God to fill me with awe and wonder today?
How did that awe and wonder today make me closer to God?
In what ways was my awe like Mary's today?

CHAPTER THREE

according to your word

The Prayer of Assent to God

The angel said to her, "The Holy Spirit will come upon you, and...overshadow you; therefore the child to be born will be holy; he will be called the Son of God...for nothing will be impossible with God." Then Mary said, "Here am I, the servant of the Lord; let it be with me according to your word."

Luke 1:35-38

∽

The scene: Mary and Gabriel continue their astonishing dialogue at the spring of Nazareth.

∽

O God,
thank you for your perfect will.
Let your will be done for me. Amen

Mary's assent to Gabriel—and ultimately to God—changed the course of human history forever. What if she had said "No"? Would God have *forced* her to be the bearer of the Messiah? Probably not: God has always wanted children, not slaves. Would God have looked for another worthy virgin or perhaps even postponed the birth of the Savior until another age? We'll never know, because Mary *did* assent. Her "Here am I" means she consented to her calling from God, cooperating with grace and accepting salvation not only for herself, but for all humankind. Both Samuel and Isaiah said "Here am I" when God called them; Mary echoed the greatest of the prophets in her acquiescence.

Mary agreed to "let it be with me according to your word." Her answer sounds easy, almost careless. But that answer was based on her knowledge of and devotion to God and God's grace. Gabriel had already said, "You have found favor with God." This meant that Mary had both a quality of holiness about her and enough wisdom to parent the Son of God. Here was a young woman who loved God with all her heart and mind and strength and soul, and God called her just as he called Abraham and Paul—and as God is calling you, today.

Trust: Praying as God's Servant

When Mary called herself "the servant of the Lord," she was saying, "I don't belong to myself. I belong to the Lord. My decisions depend on the will of God." She *didn't* say, "Well, all right. I'm constrained to do this. I'll slave away for God." Calling herself God's servant meant instead that she trusted God, and the only action she had to take after her prayer of assent was *to do nothing*. Because she trusted, God did it all.

Trust is simple, but not easy. If Adam and Eve had trusted God, they wouldn't have sinned by eating forbidden fruit; if we humans truly trusted God, we would quit fighting for what we desire, waiting instead for God to give it to us. Bigotry, fear, and anger can all spring from failure to trust God. Fear of losing control over one's life or finances or spouse or business can make people sick both mentally and spiritually, because it arises from lack of trust.

In the encounter groups of the '60s, people were blindfolded and led by others through a building or park as a trust exercise. Or they allowed themselves to fall backward into the arms of another person whom they had to trust to catch them. These were often useful learning games for those who needed to learn trust. But the exercise we need most isn't just learning to trust others; we have to learn to trust *God* as Mary did. Human beings are

according to your word

weak and imperfect: they may let you fall blindfolded to the floor, or fall themselves while trying to prop you up. But God is powerful, able to bear your burdens, and—as Mary has shown us—God never fails.

How do you learn to trust God? If you recall the story of the prophet Gideon (Judges 6, 7, and 8), you'll remember that he insisted the person who appeared to him prove he was God or an angel of God. God had to consume a sacrifice, wet a wool fleece on a dry night, dry the fleece on a wet night, and rout an army just to gain Gideon's trust. Zechariah wanted that same kind of proof from Gabriel—and was struck dumb for it. I still hear of people who say they "put out a fleece" before the Lord, in imitation of Gideon. I wonder whether they remember that we already have the ultimate proof of God in Jesus Christ. We no longer have to look for evidence because we have the testimony of God's own life on earth. God is proved forever in the personhood, sacrifice, and resurrection of Christ.

Learning to Trust God

Trust means relinquishing control, and you learn trust by performing acts of trust. Does that mean you should go lie down in a field and presume that God will keep you from being rained upon? Of course not; that would be presuming on God's indulgence. But relinquishing control *does* mean that you can quit trying so hard to manage your whole life (and maybe your family members' or friends' lives) and let God carry the major part of the weight.

The Twelve-Step programs that have helped millions of people overcome their addictions to alcohol, narcotics, food, or other compulsions begin the steps by first, admitting helplessness, and second, calling on God for help. Just as Mary chose to be helpless or non-controlling in her conception of Jesus, submitting herself to God's help, you can choose to "let go and let God," as the old axiom suggests. To do so is not only an imitation of the Blessed Virgin, it's also an embrace of Jesus' words to God in Gethsemane, "Not what I want but what you want" (Matthew 26:39).

You may find that it's really a *relief* to surrender to God. Did you ever resign from a group or decline an office you had thought you wanted? Remember how relieved you felt afterward? You knew you had done the right thing for yourself, and probably for the organization.

Surrender of control is harder before it's done than afterward; once you say, for instance, "God, I'll quit striving so hard to make money, or get elected to that office, or make the church (or my boss or spouse or kids) listen to me. I'll trust you for it," you'll probably feel a sense of serenity.

You'll know you did the right thing when you find yourself full of peace and contentment instead of anxiety.

Living in Trust

Trust means *belief.* In order to let God take over your future, you must have faith. Saint Paul wrote,

> Do not worry about anything, but in everything by prayer and supplication with thanksgiving let your requests be made known to God. And the peace of God, which surpasses all understanding, will guard your hearts and your minds (Philippians 4:6-7).

When we pray we must pray with trust. Just as Mary lived the answer to her prayer "Let it be with me according to your word," so all of us have to live our faith, live the answers to our prayers, and believe that God will give us the peace that Saint Paul wrote about.

Imagine God's angels, girded with swords and guarding your tranquility: this is the kind of protection you get when you relinquish control over your life, trust God, and say with Mary, "Let it be with me according to your word."

Embracing God's Word

Mary's response to the angel did not mean that she was *resigned* to God's will. She is not one who has finally given up, surrendered to an enemy, or submitted to punishment. Mary's attitude wasn't that of cringing compliance: she *embraced* the plan God had for her life.

Notice that she used the term "according to your word." What word? She didn't say "your *words,*" which would have meant, "Very well, Gabriel, I'll do as you say." There's only one time in religious life when we use the singular, *word,* that way: that's when we're referring to God's Word. It isn't an accident that at Mass, the lector says at the end of the reading, "The Word of the Lord."

Mary, knowing that Gabriel's words were God's Word, was calling up the Word of creation God spoke into the blackness of chaos, the Word that still echoes so that new galaxies and stars and pulsars are created every day. The Word of God became the Word made flesh as Jesus Christ, and Mary was willing to live for him even before he was conceived. God's *Word* is God's perfect *will,* and the created universe doesn't resist it.

God's Word isn't just for the universe, nor is it limited to saints and saviors. You can embrace God's Word for *you* just as Mary did. This means devoting yourself to hearing that Word when God speaks, meditating in silence, listening in prayer, and disciplining yourself as Mary did to become fit for the kingdom.

You have not been chosen to bear the Son of God. But you *have* been called for something, not only to do something—such as being a religious or raising children or writing a book—but also to *be* a particular sort of person. You can always discern people who have answered God's call, because their personalities show it. When you pray daily, "Let it be with me according to your word," you're opening yourself up to the Spirit, and the Spirit gives you new life. You won't be less yourself; you'll be you in new three-dimensional, full-color ways.

Robbers in Our Midst

Jesus said that a person's enemies would be of their own household (Matthew 10:36), and it's the foe within who can do more damage even than Satan and his angels. If there's a little robber in you—a doubter who wants to steal your trust and destroy your confidence in God—you must seek it out and come to terms with it. Some of these psychological robbers say, "Called? You? Don't be a fool. You aren't worthy of God's calling." Others whisper, "Well, prayer is fine, but it's going to take more than that." And still others say, "You can't trust God. What about the time you prayed for help and didn't get it?"

No matter what kinds of negative thoughts go on in your head, they have no power unless you give it. You wouldn't sacrifice God's dreams for you to old ideas you've collected any more than you'd cast pearls before swine. No matter how terrible your childhood was, you're an adult now. How you live your life is up to you. You need to ask God to show you all the negativity that keeps you from wholeness. Ask Christ to redeem that negativity so that, like him, you can have a complete relationship with God.

Praying the Words

Begin the assent to God with your mind. Turn your attitude toward the Lord, remembering God's promise to Julian of Norwich that "all shall be well." God's will for you is benevolent, not angry or punishing. God is *for* you, loving you as if you were an only, cherished, and favored child. You may have to spend some time in prayer and meditation, remedying old hurts you imagined God had inflicted upon you and teaching yourself to trust again.

The second step is to take action *before* using the prayer. Begin behaving in a trusting way: make no decision, even a small one, without asking for God's guidance. Pray for protection when you turn your key in the car, and thank God for that protection when you arrive at your destination. Do nothing without God's direction and involvement.

Finally, when you find yourself leaning toward God in a new way, begin praying Mary's words of assent every morning when you waken. When you hear the alarm go off or the children running through the house, keep your eyes closed long enough to say, "Here am I, your servant, God. Let it be with me according to your word."

If you mean it, you'll feel some trepidation: it isn't easy, especially in a society that preaches taking care of Number One, to abdicate that caretaking. But you won't suffer from neglect; God will care for you in the same way that God cared for Mary when she prayed those words. And your usefulness to your family and friends, to your workplace, and to the wounded world in which you live will be multiplied a thousandfold through your surrender.

living her words

O God, teach me to pray as Mary did,
with calm trust and loving assent.
I know that your will for me is good,
and I turn myself toward you
believing that wherever you take me,
I can do your will on earth.
Here am I, your servant, God;
let it be done to me according to your word.
To Christ, to you, and to the Holy Spirit
be all honor and glory. Amen

1. Journal Your Associations

In your journal, write some associations you have with the following words or phrases: *God's will, Christ in me, trust, goodness, willingness, yes.*

2. List Your Qualities

Although you cannot give physical birth to Jesus Christ, you must give birth to him in your *life*. List some qualities that Christ's living in you will display in your personality.

3. Think About Obedience

Find an ordinary rock and put it in your bedroom or someplace where you'll see it early in the morning. Think of the ways that rock has been obedient to God and how much more life you will have through your assent to God.

4. Meditate

Meditate on the Scripture for this chapter, and find a word or phrase in it you can use as a breath prayer for the next week. To pray your breath prayer, spend a few quiet moments saying the phrase to yourself while becoming aware of your slow breathing. Then continue to repeat your word or phrase, letting the prayer take the rhythm of your breathing. You can repeat this prayer many times throughout the day; try also to pray for a longer time in the morning and at night.

reflections

*Did I become aware today that God might be calling me to do
  something?*
How did I become aware of God's call?
Am I doing what God asked me to do today?
Do I have the courage to assent to God in all things?
In what ways can my obedience be more like Mary's?

CHAPTER FOUR

my soul magnifies the lord

The Prayer of Perfect Praise

"My soul magnifies the Lord,
and my spirit rejoices in God my Savior,
for he has looked with favor on the lowliness of his servant.
Surely, from now on all generations will call me blessed;
for the Mighty One has done great things for me,
and holy is his name.
His mercy is for those who fear him
from generation to generation.
He has shown strength with his arm;
he has scattered the proud in the thoughts of their hearts.
He has brought down the powerful from their thrones,
and lifted up the lowly;
he has filled the hungry with good things,
and sent the rich away empty.
He has helped his servant Israel,
in remembrance of his mercy,
according to the promise he made to our ancestors,
to Abraham and to his descendants forever."

Luke 1:46-55

The scene: Elizabeth's and Zechariah's house was in Ain Karim, a village in the hill country a few miles from Jerusalem. Mary would have entered through the main gate into the inner courtyard, similar to an atrium, where most household work took place.

O God,
I bless you and thank you for your gift
of our Lord Jesus Christ to the world. Amen

Three remarkable things happened in a very short space of time (see Luke 1:41-55).

First, Elizabeth's unborn son leaped in her womb, and she cried out, "Blessed are you among women, and blessed is the fruit of your womb" (1:41-42).

Next she called Mary "the mother of my Lord," adding, "Blessed is she who believed that there would be a fulfillment of what was spoken to her by the Lord" (1:43,45).

And third, Mary, a village girl, began a hymn of praise that theologians have marveled over for its insights and language (1:46-55). We call this extraordinary hymn the Magnificat.

Someone could write a whole book, representing years of research and theological speculation, just on Elizabeth's speeches to Mary, perhaps even just on the phrase, "Blessed is she who believed." But even greater than Elizabeth's words are Mary's words, perhaps the greatest words of praise ever written down—words you can make your own when you use them as a personal prayer.

Magnifying the Lord

An old American hymn, "Jerusalem, My Happy Home," says that in heaven, our Lady sings the Magnificat. Mary's hymn of praise to God is considered, even by the Reformers, to be so perfect that it's worthy of eternity.

Mary's praise in the Magnificat is perfect because she names the "great things" God has done for *her*, including looking with favor on her lowliness. Because of God's goodness, she predicts that from that day, all generations would call her "blessed." But Mary's prayer of praise goes much further than this. Her Magnificat is perfect not just because of what God has done for her, but also because of what God has done throughout human history. She discerns the holiness of God and God's mercy, power, and strength. She recalls God's acts beginning with Abraham and his descendants. This is a very Jewish way of praising God—to go back to the beginning of the covenant.

It is impossible *not* to praise God when we look at that history, with its miracles of parting seas and manna in the desert, and with the greater miracles within human beings themselves: abject cowards made strong and brave, women leading armies and singing them to victory, poor speakers becoming powerful leaders, proud and conceited men learning the lessons of humility, shy shepherd boys slaying giants and becoming kings, depressed prophets being so lifted in spirit that they go in fiery glory to heaven. God's greatest pleasure seems to be making silk purses out of sow's ears, lifting up the humble, and putting profound words into ordinary mouths.

With God in our lives, nothing is ordinary. God turns things upside down and backward, so that the last are first and the proud are scattered. Mary prophesies to us a transformation of society's values, so that the hungry are finally filled with good things while the rich no longer have power over them; in fact, the rich who run the world feel empty and powerless on the Day of the Lord.

Most of all, Mary's hymn reminds us that God has remembered mercy and kept promises made two thousand years before her time, just as God is keeping the promises made through Jesus to us, two thousand years later. Our souls, like hers, cannot but cry thanks and glorify the Lord.

The Rejoicing Spirit

Mary's spirit was pure and unspotted by the world. She didn't have the negativity that infects and turns aside so many believers. Instead, she was able to let her spirit exult in unblemished adoration.

Much of her hymn echoes or enlarges on the hymn of Hannah, who prayed thanksgiving for her son in 1 Samuel 2:1-10. Both begin by exulting in God; where Hannah says, "My strength is exalted in my God," Mary says, "My spirit rejoices in God my Savior." Both women recall the mighty deeds done by God throughout the covenant. Both women point out that God cares for the poor: Hannah speaks of raising the poor from the dust and the needy from the ash heap, and Mary says that God lifts up the lowly. Both mention the deposing of the great: Hannah says the bows of the mighty are broken, and Mary says God brings the world's powerful down from their thrones. But while Hannah rejoices in her victory over her enemies, Mary speaks of God as Savior.

God the Savior

David, Mary's ancestor, was one of the first to speak of God as "a savior;" he uttered these words in 2 Samuel 22:3, shortly before his death. The kind of savior he speaks of is one who delivers from the enemy. In 2 Kings 13:5, the writer speaks of God's giving Israel a military savior who delivers Israel from the king of Aram. God is called Savior in Psalm 106:21, which is a confession of Israel's sins, and in which the author recalls God as having delivered the people from Egypt. And the prophet Jeremiah mourns God's absence, crying, "O hope of Israel, its savior in time of trouble, why should you be like a stranger in the land, like a traveler turning aside for the night?" (14:8).

The prophet Isaiah spoke frequently of the savior: God will send a savior into Egypt (Isaiah 19:20); or God calls himself Savior, most notably in Isaiah 43:3, where God, speaking through the prophet, says, "I am the Lord your God, the Holy One of Israel, your Savior." In Isaiah's prophecies, God as Savior was always in the future.

But as Mary spoke her praise to Elizabeth, the Savior was a reality, even though he was still an unborn child in Mary's womb. The people who had walked in darkness were about to have heavenly light bursting upon them; the sin of Adam and Eve could have no more power over those who believed. Saint Paul says, "For since death came by a human being [Adam], the resurrection of the dead has also come through a human being; for as all die in Adam, so all will be made alive in Christ" (1 Corinthians 15:21-22), and, "Therefore just as one man's trespass led to condemnation for all, so one man's act of righteousness leads to justification and life for all" (Romans 5:18).

God the Savior is not God the angry judge; Jesus came as one final and perfect sacrifice for the sin of the world and asks only faithfulness, trust, and belief: in other words, what Christ asks, our Mother, Mary, gave even before Christ was born.

The Savior is a deliverer not only from the grip of sin, but from the power of death. Saint Paul said that death reigned from Adam to Moses, even over those whose sins were trivial compared to Adam's (see Romans 5:14). And after Moses, the law required specific sacrifices for every kind of sin and guilt, culminating every year in the Day of Atonement, to stave off death. A faithful Jew had to remember 630 laws to be obedient *every day*. But in Jesus Christ, the Son of Mary, the law is fulfilled and the sacrifice is made once and forever for our salvation. We are redeemed by the issue of a young Virgin whose spirit rejoiced in God her savior.

All Generations of Women

Women especially have always called Mary "blessed."

In his encyclical *The Mother of the Redeemer*, Pope John Paul II says that Mary's "exceptional pilgrimage of faith represents a constant point of reference for the Church, for individuals and for communities, for peoples and nations, and in a sense for all humanity." Mary, as Mediatrix and

Mother, is a gift to all humanity, but her benefaction to women is immeasurable.

Harriet Harrison Merry says that because she has Mary as her model, she never doubts that her womanhood is included in every word of Scripture and liturgy. In terms perhaps difficult for many men to understand, Mary opens the door of faith and joy to every woman, present and future, by saying, "for henceforth all generations shall call me blessed." Mary, in the midst of a patriarchal society, is the wedge that opens a door to every woman's true liberation in God.

Mary's Magnificat foretells the meaning of the coming of Jesus, especially for all those who suffer injustice. Jesus would have two natures, one human and the other divine. Mary would be the one who trained the human personality. Because of her friendship with her son, he would become the great liberator, speaking to women as the equals of men, offering them insights into the kingdom of heaven and allowing them at the scene of his Resurrection. As Mary sings her prayer of perfect praise, she prophesies to all generations of struggling women, abused and oppressed by men or prevented by their culture from participating fully in life. "You will suffer," her prayer whispers to every girl child, "but look at me, see what a woman was meant to be, and find strength." //

Judaeo-Christian history is full of the stories of oppressed women. They suffered, yet God lifted them up and gave them honor and new courage. Jacob's first wife, Leah, had a dreary existence. She married Jacob through her father's deception (read Genesis 29:21-25), and to make matters worse, Jacob did not love her, though she bore him many children. He took her sister Rachel as his second wife and was madly in love with her.

Genesis 29:31 says, "When the Lord saw that Leah was unloved, he opened her womb; but Rachel was barren." Leah faithfully produced sons— and then watched as Jacob lavished his love on Joseph, the boy Rachel finally bore.

But God rewarded Leah's life of unswerving goodness. Her son Levi was the ancestor of Moses, and her son Judah was the first in the line of David, Solomon, and finally, Jesus Christ. Leah, a suffering and neglected woman, was pivotal in the history of Judaism and Christianity. Though she was a woman suffering in a patriarchal society, she was also the instrument of bringing Christ into that society and into a world that so badly needs his message of justice and mercy, love and equality. His message took its human shape from his experiences in the home of his mother, Mary. For this reason women of all backgrounds and times have a reason to rejoice.

Men too are heirs of Mary's prophecy of liberation for all people. They are included in the company of Mary, and they too call her blessed. By a robust relationship with the Virgin Mary, a man can experience and express himself through his feminine side, learning tenderness and receptivity in a world that usually rewards the macho individual. Some consider public devotion unmasculine, and many believe that expressing joy in God is for women only. But a man is also open to receiving God's grace. Through that receptivity, he can participate in Mary's blessedness. Thus Mary has become the prototype of all believers. Because Mary opened the door, all generations can call *us* blessed, for we all, men and women alike, have received the gift of eternal life by the merits and suffering of Jesus Christ. As we pray with Mary, we thank God for blessing us with freedom and salvation.

Raising the Lowly

The first part of Mary's prayer of praise is *personal*. Now she moves to a *social* prayer, foretelling the impact of God's sudden mercy on the common poor people around her, in a country that is groaning under the heel of foreign oppression. God will scatter the proud in the thoughts of their hearts, she says, knowing that the proud—the Herods, the Pilates, the Roman rulers—will be trapped by their own ideas about what should and should not be. Life is not fair, but God is just. The goal of the truly Christian society that God is about to create will be justice.

Sometimes, stunned by the injustice of contemporary life, we may fear that God has abandoned the world. Drug lords have overpowered rulers in some countries. In our own land, it sometimes looks as if our elected officials are more interested in their re-election than in improving the plight of the *anawim,* or downtrodden, or homeless. Children die or suffer from abuse, men beat their wives, the forests are stripped and the waters polluted, the innocent are deprived while the wicked prosper. One nation is inundated by heavy rains and flooding rivers, while another is so dry that its people can't grow food. And none of this is new: conditions were the same when Mary sang her hymn.

But God nudges human hearts to serve each other. Our duty—and the duty of all Christians—is to alleviate these problems by intense and devoted prayer followed by good works. God doesn't need servants but human beings do. One miraculous change wrought by Christ in society is our longing to serve one another. When somebody works to stop child abuse, lobbies the government to aid the poor, or protests the destruction

my soul magnifies the lord

of ancient forests, those people are helping to create the kingdom of God on earth. They are lifting up the lowly and scattering the powerful in the fantasies they've constructed for themselves. Jesus said that no one who "gives even a cup of cold water to one of these little ones…will lose their reward" (Matthew 10:42). Let your prayer be like Mary's: God "lifts up the lowly." Then add charitable works to your prayers.

The Promises He Made Our Ancestors

It doesn't matter if your genealogy is Irish or Chinese or Native American: if you are a Christian, Abraham and Sarah are your foreparents by adoption, and the promises God made to them are for you. God promised Abraham's descendants a Messiah, a Savior. Through the prophet Isaiah, God said, "He will come and save you" (Isaiah 35:4).

This promise, fulfilled in Jesus Christ, doesn't sound startling to us now. We're used to it, and it is fulfilled. Yet the world is replete with people who don't know the promise, whose lives are so bleak they can't grasp the idea that God will save them. Millions believe that they're alone in the world, without hope or friendship, not realizing that God is walking beside them. And millions more don't understand the promise: they think they have to *work* their way to heaven, not knowing that Christ is always standing by to save them. Our lives, inspired by Mary's joyful celebration of God's mercy and justice, are a witness to a world suffering the lack of God's love. Through that witness, all people can become heirs to the promises God fulfilled through Mary.

living her words

Mary's hymn is perfect praise, and you can make it your own prayer. First, read the prayer every day until you have it memorized:

> "My soul magnifies the Lord,
>   and my spirit rejoices in God my Savior,
> for he has looked with favor on the lowliness of his servant.
>   Surely, from now on all generations will call me blessed;
> for the Mighty One has done great things for me,
>   and holy is his name.
> His mercy is for those who fear him
>   from generation to generation.
> He has shown strength with his arm;
>   he has scattered the proud in the thoughts of their hearts.
> He has brought down the powerful from their thrones,
>   and lifted up the lowly;
> he has filled the hungry with good things,
>   and sent the rich away empty.
> He has helped his servant Israel,
>   in remembrance of his mercy,
> according to the promise he made to our ancestors,
>   to Abraham and to his descendants forever."
>
> Luke 1:46-55

When you have read this prayer every day for a week, begin writing in your journal some or all of the following:

1. Magnify the Lord

Offer praise for what God *is*, and describe some of the awe-inspiring works that God has wrought in the universe: galaxies, nebulae, planets, and the creation that still burgeons throughout the earth. Compare humans with their frailties to God, and give thanks that God does not have those flaws.

2. Rejoice in Christ Your Savior

Give thanks for your salvation, and recall the prayer that is said during the Stations of the Cross: *We praise you O Lord and we bless you, for by your holy cross you have redeemed the world.* Jot down the qualities about Jesus Christ that you love the most.

3. Offer Thanks

Express gratitude for all you have received, including your baptism, home, heat, food, and anything else you can think of. Then make a list of people whom you hope will call you "blessed:" your children, your co-workers, your spouse. Decide what you can do for these people.

4. Pray for Justice in the World

Pray that the justice of God's kingdom will be a reality here and now. Write what your part may be in bringing that justice to fruition. Can you be God's instrument in filling the hungry with good things? How can you show God's mercy to the broken world around you?

5. Appreciate Your Baptism

Thank God for the promises made at your baptism, which are fulfilled in your life as you learn to know Christ.

reflections

How did I magnify God today?
When I say the Magnificat, do I find more life?
How does Mary help me enter into that life?

CHAPTER FIVE

why have you treated me this way?

The Prayer of Intimate Confrontation

Assuming that he was in the group of travelers, they went a day's journey. Then they started to look for him among their relatives and friends. When they did not find him, they returned to Jerusalem to search for him. After three days they found him in the temple, sitting among the teachers, listening to them and asking them questions....When his parents saw him they were astonished; and his mother said to him, "Child, why have you treated us like this?"

Luke 2:44-48

∞

The scene: Jerusalem was a rowdy and dangerous city for a young boy. Mary and Joseph found Jesus in an outer court of the Temple (where a woman might have been allowed to enter). In such a Temple court, scholars and rabbis conducted continuous teachings on the Law and the Prophets.

∞

God,
I don't always understand you,
or life, or why you let us suffer.
Grant me the grace to speak to you honestly
and to trust you with my life. Amen

Jesus was, after all, twelve years old when his parents discovered he was missing—old enough to be considered a grown man by some first-century Palestinian standards. And a number of scholars believe that when the family visited Jerusalem for Passover, Jesus made his bar mitzvah—which made him a man in Judaism—at the synagogue connected to the Outer Temple.

But on the way home, his parents' discovery that he wasn't with the other young people in the crowd from Nazareth and that nobody had seen him for at least twenty-four hours probably made them frantic, regardless of Jesus' status as a semi-adult.

Jerusalem, much like some of our modern cities, was full of dangers, especially for innocent, countrified Galilean boys. Opium-laced wine was sold not only in taverns but on street corners. Men sought teenage boys for immoral purposes, sometimes forcing them onto ships where they were taken as male prostitutes into brothels or pagan temples in faraway cities. Knifings, Zealot riots, insurrections, trampling by Roman horses—all these were common occurrences in greater Jerusalem.

When Mary finally found Jesus, he was involved in a leisurely argument with the scholars, probably over a Torah passage. Three days' looking for her son, with no sleep and little thought of eating or resting, had left Mary anxious and high-strung. Maybe even unreasonable.

"Son," she cried, "why have you done this to us?"

Confrontation and Intimacy

Intimacy breeds honesty. If you're like most people, you don't have confrontations with strangers or casual acquaintances. You save your honesty for those who matter most to you—your spouse, your kids, your siblings, or a very close friend. You say things to an intimate other in your life that you would *never* say to anyone else—good words, words of love and affection, and some words that are utterly negative, charged with anger and unhappiness.

"You never listen to me!" a woman shouts at her husband. This woman works in a bank and deals diplomatically with difficult customers, but when she gets home she feels safe to say what she thinks, and her public personality no longer hides her true feelings.

Loving someone and letting them love you means that walls have to come down and curtains must open. You have to be as willing to fight sometimes as you are to be affectionate.

Can you imagine getting as upset at someone you see occasionally at

why have you treated me this way?

church as you do at a family member? Of course not. And when Mary found Jesus, she felt entitled to speak to him frankly about her anger and her fearful experience—not as to a stranger, but as mother to son. "Why have you treated us this way?" she cried, right in front of the scholars.

Confronting God

"I know I'm not supposed to get mad at God," I once heard a woman say, and I knew she spoke for many other Christians. But wait a minute! *Where* does it say you can't be angry at God? What verse of Scripture tells you God doesn't tolerate your real feelings? This is the same God who told Moses, Job, and Isaiah,"Come now, let us argue it out" (Isaiah 1:18).

Perhaps the best example of confronting God we have in modern times is in the musical *Fiddler on the Roof.* The leading character, Tevye, constantly talks to God—arguing, questioning, complaining, and praising. His very breath is filled with words to God, and all through the play he asks, in one way or another, "Why have you treated me this way?" God is very real for Tevye. The Russian Jew considers God a friend, an enemy, a parent, and a complaint department.

You can talk to God the same way, because God never reacts with anger to honest speech. When you confront God, it's a sign of your intimacy with God. *God already knows* when you're angry or frustrated or defeated, so why not say so in prayer?

If you're unemployed and you've been praying for a job for a year, if your kids are drinking, skipping school, and driving you crazy in spite of the pleas you've made to God, if you had to put your aging father—a brilliant man until Alzheimer's started destroying his mind—in a nursing home, if your best friend borrowed your car, your perfume, and finally your spouse—you're undoubtedly angry and depressed. So tell God. So ask, "Why have you treated me this way? Why didn't you help me?" If you feel as if God doesn't love you any more, *say so.* God can't break through to you if you won't break your silence. So when you quit talking, you're not being intimate with the God who made you and sent Jesus to give his life for you.

Does this sound heretical? Then you haven't read the Psalms lately. Listen:

> Why, O Lord, do you stand far off?
> Why do you hide yourself in times of trouble?...
> But you do see! Indeed you note trouble and grief.
> Psalm 10:1,14

And how about,

> How long, O Lord? Will you forget me forever?
> How long will you hide your face from me?
> How long must I bear pain in my soul,
>   and have sorrow in my heart all day long?
> How long shall my enemy be exalted over me?
> Consider and answer me, O Lord my God!
>
> Psalm 13:1-3

These verses from the Psalms are only two examples from Scripture in which the writer is complaining about life. People in the Bible grieve, fight, become angry, and generally act like human beings; and they tell God how they feel.

When Anger Is Sin

Saint Paul writes, "Be angry but do not sin; do not let the sun go down on your anger, and do not make room for the devil" (Ephesians 4:26-27).

Anger itself is no sin; it's what you do about it that can lead to evil. Anger that leads to abuse, anger that treats others unfairly, or anger that's held inside can be sinful. All kinds of devils go on the attack when you nurse a grudge. Saint Paul knew what he was talking about: his own anger at the Christians led him to help in the stoning of Stephen. It enabled him to persecute God's people—until Christ met him on the road to Damascus.

Bitterness and anger can tear families apart, destroy marriages, turn children and parents against each other, and demolish friendships. But the anger that has this kind of power isn't the sudden wrath that leads you to confront someone; it's the anger that you bury until it festers and spoils inside you that can ruin a relationship.

Unexpressed anger at God can be destructive to your faith! Yet every day that the sun rises, someone gets mad at God—and lets the same sun set on that wrath. A man or woman who wouldn't go to bed mad at their spouse or kids can fall into a fitful sleep every night for *months* because they won't say to God, "Why have you done this to me?"

Achieving Intimacy with God

I know a man who walks six miles to his job every day so he can "chat with God," to use his words. For this man, God is more than real; God is his closest, most intimate companion. He talks to God about the weather, the world situation, his wife and daughter, his breakfast—in other words, anything he would talk about to a good friend. When he broke his toe and had to be driven to work, he was frustrated and almost disoriented because he didn't have that hour-long walk and talk with the Lord.

You can achieve any level of intimacy with God that you desire—but you've got to be honest. You've got to be willing to say "Why have you done this to me?" as easily as you say "I love you."

living her words

Try the following two-part quiz:

Part One

1. Have you recently lost someone you loved (through death, divorce, abandonment, moving, or any other way)?
2. Are you unemployed or underemployed?
3. Are your children misbehaving?
4. Do you have responsibility for aging parents?
5. Is your primary relationship less than deeply satisfying?
6. Do you dislike your home?
7. Are you lonely?
8. Do you think your talents are not appreciated?

Part Two

1. Do you have physical problems that might be worsened by stress, such as asthma, arthritis, or indigestion?
2. Do you find yourself avoiding private prayer or rushing to get through?
3. Are you having a flat experience at Mass?
4. Has anyone noticed that you're grouchy or short-tempered?
5. Do tears come to your eyes for almost no reason?
6. Have you remained bitter about something for a while?
7. Is your anger at God getting pretty close to the surface?
8. Do you wonder why God answers some people's prayers but seems to ignore yours?
9. Are you suffering from vague feelings of guilt?
10. Do you think God is unfair?

Take a look at your answers. If you answered even one question in the first part with a "yes," you may have reasons for some anger. If you had two "yes" answers in part two, that anger may be making you sick—and leading you to sin.

reflections

Was I completely honest with God today?
How has lack of intimacy with God kept me from real life?
How can Mary's example help me be more honest?

CHAPTER SIX

i have been searching for you anxiously

The Prayer of Longing

"[Your father and] I have been searching for you in great anxiety."
Luke 2:48

The scene: Mary continues to address her son in the Temple, after he has been lost for three days and has finally turned up in the company of rabbis and scholars, who were amazed at his questions and answers. Jesus says to Mary, "Didn't you know I would be about my Father's business?" But his parents don't understand what he means.

Dear Christ,
teach me to long for you with the same fervor
with which your Mother searched for you in Jerusalem.
Amen

In the last chapter, we saw our Lord's Mother expressing her unhappiness with Jesus, saying "Why have you treated me this way?" That disquietude with Jesus rose from love and intimacy; now she tells him how much he matters to her and how great was her fear that he was gone forever. The phrase "with great anxiety" probably doesn't even touch on the desperation she felt, but her words imply, "I would not have stopped until I found you."

Jesus answered, "Did you not know that I must be in my Father's house?" (Luke 2:49).

And Scripture adds, "But they did not understand what he said to them" (Luke 2:50).

Remember that when Mary spoke to Jesus she was speaking not only to her twelve-year-old son but also to God Incarnate. She expressed the longing we all feel for God at times, and there are no words God would rather hear.

If you glimpse what life would be like *without* God, you know what Mary went through. What if her child had disappeared forever? Children were abducted in those days—just as they are now—and either sold into slavery or abused and killed. Any parent whose child has disappeared or is just much too late coming home knows the terrible fear that must have gripped our Lord's Mother. Had he been kidnapped or killed? *Where* was Jesus?

Reasons for the Search

Do you ever feel as if God's presence is slipping away? Maybe nothing is really wrong, but you discover that the divine person of whom you were once aware within your heart seems distant or even absent. Perhaps God is daring you to follow, to pursue and seek. Whatever prayer and sacramental activities are part of your life, probably the holiest thing you can do is to chase God. Some of our greatest saints have suggested that God sometimes moves out of our spiritual sight. Sometimes these saints felt abandoned or as if God were unattainable. But they learned that at times like these, God is only flirting.

At other times, you know God's action and presence in your life—but you want more than you've had. You want to see God face to face, to know Jesus Christ not only as your Savior but also as the Bridegroom of the Church. Perhaps your pattern of prayer no longer feels as if it's enough. You're like the children in C.S. Lewis's *The Chronicles of Narnia* who go to heaven, Aslan's Country, in the last volume. They keep shouting, "Inward and upward!" because they desire more, more of God.

Or maybe your life has gone so badly of late that you wonder if God is busy somewhere else. Perhaps your spouse has died or left you. Perhaps you've lost your job, or your teenager has violently rebelled. Maybe you have an aging parent who's sick or dying. Maybe your doctor has given you news about your own health that has frightened you. If you are suffering with more than one kind of trouble and things keep getting worse, you could finally believe that God just plain doesn't care.

Whatever your situation, when you finally think God can hear you, you may cry, "I've been searching for you with great anxiety." And there are no words God would rather hear.

Expressing Your Longing

No words are more welcome to God than "I have been searching for you." Add "with great anxiety" and you've told God how much you care.

Most of the time, the prayers God hears are pleas for help. There's certainly nothing wrong with that; God has instructed us to pray for what we need. Our Lord Jesus Christ said, "Ask, and it will be given you; search, and you will find; knock, and the door will be opened for you. For everyone who asks receives, and everyone who searches finds, and for everyone who knocks, the door will be opened" (Matthew 7:7-8).

But God would like to hear something besides requests. Imagine the joy in heaven when God hears, "I've been searching for you."

Look at David, Psalmist and King of Israel and Judah. God loved him, yet at times, David sensed the mystery of God's greatness and the emptiness that comes with God's apparent absence. No wonder, then, that one of David's greatest Psalms says,

As a deer longs for flowing streams,
    so my soul longs for you, O God.
My soul thirsts for God,
    for the living God.
When shall I come and behold
    the face of God?
My tears have been my food
    day and night,
while people say to me continually,
    "Where is your God?"
                                Psalm 42:1-3

David speaks here with two themes. One theme is that David's adversaries taunt him, saying God doesn't exist (or won't help him), as in verse three: "My tears have been my food / day and night, / while people say to me continually, / 'Where is your God?'" David wants to prove that God is God, the Savior of Israel. His personal adversaries—those who want to overthrow the throne—*and* the nation's enemies, such as the Philistines, are jeering at him.

Second, his soul thirsts for the God he loves, as in verse four: "These things I remember, / as I pour out my soul: / how I went with the throng, / and led them in procession to the house of God, / with glad shouts and songs of thanksgiving, / a multitude keeping festival." He recalls here the day the Ark of the Covenant was borne to Jerusalem; on that day, David danced all the way to the Temple at the head of the procession, for joy of God's presence. Now, for David, that presence is far away, and he longs to know that joy again.

Those who search for God certainly aren't strangers to God! Mary lived with Jesus, the Incarnate God, from the moment of his birth, and David was God's most outspoken lover. Moses certainly had more than a shallow acquaintance with Yahweh. Though he spoke with God directly every day, still he was not satisfied until he could at least glimpse the glory of his God:

> The LORD said to Moses, "…You have found favor in my sight, and I know you by name." Moses said, "Show me your glory, I pray." And he said, "I will make all my goodness pass before you, and will proclaim before you the name, 'The LORD'; and I will be gracious to whom I will be gracious, and will show mercy on whom I will show mercy" (Exodus 33:17-19).

Even though Moses had seen great miracles, had stretched his own hand out over the sea and parted it, had heard the voice of Yahweh, he wanted more. He wanted to glimpse God's glory, whatever that means—perhaps to peep into heaven for a nanosecond, to see God on the throne. All through the Bible, we find men and women who longed to see the face of God, who searched with great anxiety.

Preparing for God

Isaiah, called in the seventh century before Christ to become prophet of Israel, *did* see God on the throne, and the sight gave him the strength to say, "Here am I."

His experience begins with the vision itself:

> In the year that King Uzziah died, I saw the Lord sitting on a throne, high and lofty; and the hem of his robe filled the temple (Isaiah 6:1).

Notice that God is high and unreachable, almost out of Isaiah's sight. What Isaiah sees is what Moses saw: God's glory. Next, he records the worship of heaven, something nobody had ever seen before:

> Seraphs were in attendance above him; each had six wings: with two they covered their faces, and with two they covered their feet, and with two they flew. And one called to another and said: "Holy, holy, holy is the Lord of hosts; the whole earth is full of his glory" (Isaiah 6:2-3).

During Mass in the Preface to the Holy, Holy, the celebrant mentions these angels who are always present at God's throne and invites us to join with them and the saints in praising God.

At the moment at which Isaiah beholds the heavenly vision, he realizes that, like all humans, he is a miserable sinner:

> The pivots on the thresholds shook at the voices of those who called, and the house filled with smoke. And I said: "Woe is me! I am lost, for I am a man of unclean lips, and I live among a people of unclean lips; yet my eyes have seen the King, the Lord of hosts!" (Isaiah 6:4-5).

As dearly as I may long to see God, I know I don't deserve to. For I am a sinner, and I live in a world full of sinners. If God appeared to me right now, I would think I had to die, because I am so unworthy. But God is always the source of more grace than we can imagine. God longs for Isaiah, just as Isaiah longs for God. So God creates a way for the prophet to be forgiven, a mysterious possibility for absolution:

> Then one of the seraphs flew to me, holding a live coal that had been taken from the altar with a pair of tongs. The seraph touched my mouth with it and said: "Now that this has touched your lips, your guilt has departed and your sin is blotted out" (Isaiah 6:6-7).

Perhaps if you feel that God is far away, it's because you're letting your sins, past or present, impede your sense of God's presence. Notice that the seraph says, "your guilt has departed;" in other words, even if Isaiah's sense of sin was mistaken, even if he was a sinless man, God lifted his sense of shame and hid his sins.

You don't have to be touched on the lips with hot coals; the Church offers the sacrament of reconciliation, in which you can confess your sins and have God's absolution delivered to you—not by a flaming creature with tongs but by a priest with the Sign of the Cross!

At the end of this vision, Isaiah can hear God calling:

> Then I heard the voice of the Lord saying, "Whom shall I send, and who will go for us?" And I said, "Here am I; send me!" (Isaiah 6:8).

Would Isaiah have taken his mission to prophesy to the people if he had not seen this vision? We'll never know. What we *do* know is that Isaiah had the experience we long for—the experience of seeing God. Because of it, he wrote prophecies of Christ that we hear with joy.

To See Thee...

Saint Thomas Aquinas also longed for the face of God. This brilliant Dominican, who wrote the *Summa Theologica*, perhaps the most comprehensive collation of systematic theology, is said to have been praying—before several witnesses—in front of the crucifix in the cathedral at Mainz, Germany. According to those witnesses, Christ spoke from the cross, tenderly asking, "What do you want, Thomas?"

Aquinas might have asked for health (for his was not good), or money for his order, or any number of physical comforts. Instead, he replied, "Thee, only; to see Thee face to face."

"I have been searching for you anxiously," Mary said, and her words are spoken by saints and prophets throughout history. Speak them yourself, and God may answer.

living her words

Mary, dearest Mother, as you searched
your heart was near to breaking. How could you live
without Him? What would a day have meant to you
without your Son in it? Mary,
dearest Mother, ask God
to teach me this same longing.

1. Read or listen

Find a recording or a copy of the music for Saint Thomas Aquinas' hymn, "Humbly I Adore Thee" (also called "God With Hidden Majesty" and "Adoro Te Devote"). If you can, play or sing it. Notice the ways that Aquinas believes Jesus is hidden from sight: behind the veil, within the host, even by his own splendor. Try to memorize the verse that most exemplifies your own search for God.

2. Meditate

Think about times when God seemed far away. Was it because you were suffering, or because you were ignoring God, or because God wanted you to seek and find? What were the circumstances of each situation? Does God seem closer or farther away now? During a time of quiet, recreate a scene in which God was far away (or use your present situation). Explain to God how anxiously you were searching (or are searching right now). Allow yourself to long for God.

3. Journal

Write a letter to God, saying, "I'm searching for you." Tell God what you want from your relationship and why you want it. Tell God about your meditation and how it made you feel.

4. List

Make a list of ways you can search for God in your ordinary day—for example, in the Mass, in nature, or in Scripture. Try to keep that spirit of searching very present in your mind; as you try to find God in each event or place, jot down the results of that experience.

---

reflections

Am I really searching for God?
What put excitement into my search today?
How does Mary's experience make me long for Christ?

CHAPTER SEVEN

they have no wine

The Prayer of Intercession

On the third day there was a wedding in Cana of Galilee, and the mother of Jesus was there. Jesus and his disciples had also been invited to the wedding. When the wine gave out, the mother of Jesus said to him, "They have no wine...." When the steward tasted the water that had become wine,...the steward called the bridegroom and said to him, "Everyone serves the good wine first, and then the inferior wine after the guests have become drunk. But you have kept the good wine until now." Jesus did this, the first of his signs, in Cana of Galilee, and revealed his glory; and his disciples believed in him.

John 2:1-3,9-11

The scene: The traditional Cana of Galilee is Kefr Kanna in the vicinity of Nazareth, where not one but two churches—one Catholic, one Greek Orthodox—claim to be built on the very site of Christ's first recorded miracle! However, modern scholars believe that the name is derived from *qana*, which means *reeds*. They think the true site should be at a ruin called Kirbet Qanah, in the green hills of lower Galilee. This plain was apparently part of Herod's domain, which explains why a *basilikos*, or royal official, was probably present at the wedding.

Lord Christ,
it was your Mother who first asked you a favor for others.
Make me the same kind of unselfish intercessor that she is
in her pleadings for the world. Amen

When you read this Scripture, you may wonder why Mary cared so much about the wine at a wedding that she asked Jesus for a miracle. Compared to such problems as Roman oppression, the corruption of the priesthood, and terrible poverty, running out of wine at a wedding may have seemed a trivial need. People can certainly live without wine—in fact, some people would be better off if they did! But by asking Jesus for help, she revealed his glory for the first time and gave us an example of *the prayer of intercession*—asking God to help someone else.

Weddings are important to God. As soon as earth is created, God makes Adam and then creates a partner for him, describing the marriage relationship as becoming one body (see Genesis 2:24). Throughout the Hebrew Scriptures, God calls himself the "husband" or "bridegroom" of Israel. Later, in several of Jesus' parables, he describes himself as the bridegroom. And the Revelation of Saint John shows us a picture of Jesus as bridegroom of the Church, with the saved of earth gathering for his wedding supper. So this was an appropriate time and place for Jesus' first miracle and Mary's first prayer of intercession.

Mary's Concern for the Bridal Couple

Our Lady's first concern must have been for the bride and bridegroom. Surely she remembered a festive betrothal that had made her Joseph's legal wife even though they had not yet lived together. About three months after the dowries and the bride price had been exchanged and the writ of marriage proclaimed by the fathers of the couple, most Galilean bridegrooms of Joseph's generation observed the ancient custom of kidnapping their brides. They came at midnight with their groomsmen; alert virgin attendants, who had stayed up late to keep the lamps trimmed, opened the doors when the bridegroom arrived. The man then whisked his wife away, while her wide-awake parents stayed out of sight. Beginning the next afternoon, the bridegroom held *his* wedding party for both families and their friends, a party that might go on for several days. Recall that it was on the *seventh* day of Samson's marriage feast that his first wife gave his men the answer to his riddle! (See Judges 14:10-18.)

Brides wore their best garments and would adorn themselves with any jewels they had; but it was the bridegroom whose clothing and demeanor were the focus of the wedding celebration. Instead of our modern song, "Here comes the bride," the cry heard throughout a city was "The bridegroom comes!" Psalm 19 compares the radiance of the sun to that of a bridegroom (verses 5-6). His joy was the community's joy.

they have no wine

We know this wasn't the bride's family's feast, because the waiter in charge went *to the bridegroom* to say that this was the choice wine. Mary couldn't have wanted the bridegroom to start his days as a husband embarrassed and in apparent poverty. Perhaps more guests than expected showed up. Or maybe it was a hot day and they drank more than usual. Or perhaps the wedding went on longer than planned. Whatever happened, the wine was gone.

The Families of the Bride and Groom

Mary's second concern was for the families. A Jewish wedding was an official exchange. A decent woman in that society was always the property of a man, and at a wedding, the switch was made from father to groom. That wedding was also the joining of families. The community of friends and relatives came together to recognize that the Bar Judahs and the Bar Jonahs were now one family: appropriate goods and money had been shuffled, the bride's dowry had been placed in trust, and the children that issued from this union would be shared in both clans' lineages.

For months, the men of those families had met and tried to discern each others' financial situations, social positions, and personalities, for they would be honor-bound to help each other in times of need. A father-in-law could be reluctant to put his daughter's husband to work if he had humiliated the family at the feast. And since the bride would usually go to live with her husband's family, a mother-in-law who was disappointed in the dowry her father had provided could make the young girl's married life difficult.

The Royal Guest

Third, a royal official was probably present (see John 4:46), so the wedding had an even more important aspect: this was an opportunity for Herodian approval of the families involved. Perhaps these were relatives of Jesus and Mary, or at least good friends. They wanted the best for this couple and their parents, and if a *basilikos* or royal representative were present, perhaps along with some of his friends, the families' social standing could rise—but not if the wine ran out and there was no money to quickly procure more!

Social status in those days meant more than reputation. It would open the door to obtaining certain jobs in the Herodian court, buying better food from royal caravans, and gaining an audience with Herod for redress of grievance or property settlement. We can even wonder if the royal official met Jesus three years later, when he came before Herod after his arrest.

The Need for Celebration

Finally, Mary knew that where her Son was present there should be celebration. Jesus himself said (in Matthew 9:15) that when the bridegroom is present, his followers do not fast. God has held up a great history of celebration to us, offering a list of feasts to be observed every year, and reminding the Israelites (in Nehemiah 8:10) not to spoil the Lord's day with weeping for their sins, because rejoicing in the Lord must be the source of all strength. In this same way, we celebrate the presence of God in the Mass and by living joyful, Christ-filled lives.

Becoming an Intercessor

Whatever other reason Mary had for her concern about the wine, she turned straight to her Son and interceded for the host. "They have no wine," she said, and in those four words, set us an example for intercessory prayer.

Chances are you won't be called upon to help furnish wine for a marriage feast (unless it's the wedding of your own child). But look around your city or town: what kinds of poverty do you see? Are some people suffering from physical hunger or medical problems they can't afford to have treated? How does your city deal with the problem of housing for the poor and unemployed?

How about emotional and spiritual hunger: do you see evidence that a great number of people are suffering from psychological or spiritual need? Perhaps you know a woman who's headed for divorce, or a childless couple who longs for a baby, or a widower who's dying of loneliness.

Maybe you live where there isn't clean air to breathe or safe water to drink. Is your community without something else? How about morality and spiritual maturity? Do you think that this entire *nation* is in need of faith in God?

Sometimes you may pray for your friends, as Mary did when the wine was gone. Sometimes you're repeating a prayer request from your church or praying for someone you've read about in the papers. Whenever you pray for others, pray in the example of our Lord's Mother, saying, "They have no...."

Turn to Jesus Christ and tell him, "They have no food, they have no

they have no wine

homes, they have no love, no children, no good water, no faith." Wherever you see a lack, you can ask Christ to fill it. If Jesus was willing to perform a miracle just for wine at a wedding, think how much more he wants to fill the hungry or stop the strife in faraway countries or help a loving couple become parents.

No prayer is too trivial, no need too small. Does your neighbor have headaches? Tell the Lord that she has no health. Does your daughter's school lack sports equipment? Tell God about it. Does your parish need a nursery attendant? You do not have because you do not ask. Is your husband impatient with your son? Turn to Jesus and say, "He has no patience."

No need is too great. When you read about countries at war, you can say to Christ, "They have no peace," and pray that he'll perform miracles. Don't be afraid to pray about anything: Mary has given us an example of going boldly with a request for help.

And when you pray, mention the name of our Lord's Mother.

When a young writer recently brought a manuscript to me for evaluation, I recognized its worth and suggested sending it to a publisher for whom I had written several books. I added, "And be sure to tell the editor I told you to send it." Calling on the name of Mary in our prayers of intercession is like my young friend mentioning me to an editor. God knows Mary, and knows her worth to the world. You might say a prayer something like this:

"O God, as Mary asked Jesus for wine at Cana, so I ask you to perform a miracle for my neighbor, who has no children. And reveal your glory through answering this prayer. I ask this in Jesus' name. Amen."

Or perhaps, if you like to be a little more formal,

"Almighty God, who granted to the Blessed Virgin Mary the answer to her prayer for wine at Cana, bless me as I imitate her in asking that you grant mercy and relief to my childless neighbor. I ask this through Jesus Christ, your Son, our Lord, who lives and reigns with you and the Holy Spirit, one God, now and forever. Amen."

Ask Mary herself to pray your prayers. I like to write my prayers of intercession in my journal, and one of them reads, "Blessed Saint Mary, who at Cana boldly told your Son that the people had no wine, pray to him for the people of my city, where there are those who have no homes." You can even make a novena for the homeless to the Blessed Mother, asking that she pray for your concerns.

Be willing also to be part of the *answer* to these prayers. Don't forget to help out by serving at your local soup kitchen, and if you can afford to, donate part of that meal. Instead of selling your *nicer* old clothes through a consignment shop, give them all to the poor. Offer to baby-sit for a distraught teenage mother. Give generously not of your excess but from your substance, to care for those in need.

The Blessed Virgin was never honored at a bridegroom's wedding feast, for when she went to live with Joseph she was already with child by the Holy Spirit. But she gained the greater honor by becoming the revelator of Christ's glory at Cana and the example for all intercessors. The great biblical story began with an earthly marriage and will end with a spiritual one, so it's appropriate that Jesus began his ministry with a wedding miracle. For what was the ultimate result of that miracle? "Jesus…revealed his glory; and his disciples believed in him" (John 2:11).

living her words

1. Pray for the World

Find a copy of today's paper, and look for stories about situations that need God's intervention—stories of poverty, or illness, or war, or crime. Cut out three of these stories, and paste them in your journal. Then, using the name of Mary in your prayer, say to God, "They have no money, food, home, etc." Spend some time in prayer, asking God to heal these situations. Pray for these people daily, for as long as God guides you to do so.

2. Pray for Those You Love

In your journal, make a list of ten people in your life who need God's help, then tell God what they lack. If possible, make a covenant to pray for these loved ones daily *for one year.* You might like to make a check on your calendar every day when you have interceded for them.

3. Meditate

Re-read the entire story of the wedding at Cana, and imagine yourself in this scene. What part do you play in the wedding or the feast? Meditate on this story for a few minutes every day for a week, and see how you are changed by it. Journal any thoughts you have about this gospel event.

reflections

What need in my community and the world most troubles me?
Will trying to relieve this situation give me more life?
How did Mary set an example for me?

do whatever he tells you

Finding Your Rule of Life

His mother said to the servants, "Do whatever he tells you."
John 2:5

∞

The scene: At the wedding party at Cana, Jesus has said that his time has not yet come, but Mary now speaks directly to the servants and wine stewards, who are waiting nearby. The wine steward usually bought the wine with money given him by the host, decanted it, and tasted it to make sure it had not turned to vinegar. He made sure it was kept cool and served properly by servants or slaves. The custom of using a wine steward at a wedding was probably borrowed from Greek and Roman cultures; today, we usually call such people *caterers*.

Mary's words to the servants can become a rule of life for Christians.

∞

O God,
thank you for Mary's trust in you.
Now make me able to do what you tell me to do. Amen

I have an acquaintance who takes God shopping. My friend doesn't pick up so much as a length of fabric for clothing or a bottle of Tabasco sauce for her Cajun recipe unless she feels a powerful inner nudging that means God has given her permission to buy it. I was intrigued by her experience, impressed that she was so in touch with God that she made shopping a spiritual experience; so I tried her method. I was in the grocery store for two hours and emerged with a jar of peanut butter—and I bought that only because I told my husband I would.

Afterward, I sat in the car for a few minutes, clutching my peanut butter and wondering why God had abandoned me in the supermarket. As I prayed for understanding, God spoke to my mind. "Now," God said, "do you want to go back in there and do what you know very well how to do?" Instantly I saw my error. *God hadn't told me to shop the way my friend does.*

Don't make my mistake. Taking on the rule of life that Mary has left us *does* mean doing whatever Christ tells us. The difference is that each individual has to listen to what God calls that person to do. We aren't all called to grocery-shop with God, nor are we instructed to fill water jars for a miracle: the servants at Cana already did that.

But the wedding at Cana does show us what obeying God is about. The miracle of the wine *revealed Christ's glory and made his disciples believe in him.* It showed the world that he was the Son of God.

That is what your life can do if you listen for God's calling. Every step you take and every word you speak can reveal the glory of Jesus Christ. In fact, that's how you'll know for sure that you're doing whatever God tells you.

Finding Your Instructions

God didn't create the world and then abandon its inhabitants. Nor does God expect you to function without any source of knowledge or help. You have six main resources.

1. The Church

The authority of the Church, the guardian of the Faith through twenty centuries, will guide you. Your participation in the sacraments is your primary act of obedience to Christ, and you can only partake of them through the corporate structure of the Church. The Church has also created a set of moral and spiritual doctrines against which you can measure anything you believe you hear Christ saying to you. You have a great reference library in the Church's writers and scholars, many of whom expound the concept of *radical obedience*, committing yourself to God without reservation. You also have the inestimable wisdom of the saints, especially Saint Augustine of Hippo who said, "Have love and do as you please." By this, Augustine meant—as Jesus did—that the person who really, truly operates out of love for God and *all* others will not sin or infringe in any way on the well-being of others.

2. Sacred Scripture

God has given you the gift of the Bible to study for inspiration and guidance. Christ will never call you to do anything that violates the Scriptures. Yes, some of our Christian practices appear to fly in the face of the law as it is presented in the Hebrew Scriptures; but remembering that Jesus *fulfilled* the law, Christians are free within the new law of love. In the Bible, you have the Ten Commandments and the Summary of the law: "'You shall love the Lord your God with all your heart, and with all your soul, and with all your mind.' This is the greatest and first commandment. And a second is like it: 'You shall love your neighbor as yourself.' On these two commandments hang all the law and the prophets" (Matthew 22:37-40). You also have the New Commandment: "I give you a new commandment, that you love one another. Just as I have loved you, you also should love one another" (John 13:34).

Some people take potluck when they read the Bible. That's the old practice of opening the Bible without looking, then placing the finger at any verse—and using that as inspiration for the day. For anyone searching for God's guidance in their life, such a practice might not be any better than trying to find God's instructions in a fortune cookie.

Instead, you might want to take the Bible more seriously as the Word of God, spending more time with it. In that case, you'll profit from reading it in bigger chunks, starting with the Gospel of John, then proceeding to Mark, Luke, and Matthew, in that order. You'll find that the New Testament epistles are full of good advice for Christian life, so begin your reading of this part of Scripture with Saint Paul's Epistle to the Romans and then the Epistle of Saint James. If you're ready for the Hebrew Scriptures, read Genesis, Exodus, and the historical books (1 Samuel through Esther). And in the Book of Psalms you'll discover a whole life of prayer! Read some of them at least once a week. When you're familiar with these books of the Scripture, go on to read the historical and prophetic books. Use a Bible commentary if you have one available.

---

3. The Holy Spirit

Remember that every baptized person is indwelt by God the Holy Spirit. Jesus said, "The Advocate, the Holy Spirit, whom the Father will send in my name, will teach you everything, and remind you of all that I have said to you" (John 14:26). The Holy Spirit is your teacher on earth. When you commit yourself to Christ every morning—you might want to use the prayer of assent that you learned in chapter 3—the Holy Spirit becomes your guide and assistant. The Holy Spirit's mission on earth is to glorify Christ and to inspire humans. The Holy Spirit quickened the writers of the Bible. The same Holy Spirit is Christ's Advocate in your life and leads you to this next resource.

4. Prayer

The fourth avenue for seeking direction is prayer. The Spirit prays within us—in fact, in *The Confession of Saint Patrick,* the saint says,

> On another night, I do not know, God knows,
> whether within me or beside me,
> in most learned words I heard those whom
> I could not yet understand,
> except that at the very end of the prayer one spoke out thus:
> "He Who has given His own soul for you
> He it is Who speaks in you,"
> and thus I was awakened rejoicing.
> And again I saw Him praying within myself...
> and there He was praying vigorously (p. 70-71).

The Holy Spirit never abandons you, and the minute you feel the need of God's guidance in any situation, that Spirit will hurry to help you. You have to *start* your prayers, but somewhere soon afterward, the Holy Spirit prays your prayer; Saint Paul says, "We do not know how to pray as we ought, but [the] Spirit intercedes.... And God, who searches the heart, knows what is the mind of the Spirit, because the Spirit intercedes...according to the will of God" (Romans 8:26-27). All you have to do is begin, and from then on, the Holy Spirit can give you the words if you need words.

Not all prayer is asking for instruction. There are prayers of praise and thanksgiving, prayers of worship and adoration, prayers of petition and intercession. Sometimes God simply wants to be with you in peaceful silence. Thousands of Christians are now using some kind of centering prayer or breath prayer. Father Thomas Keating's book *Open Heart, Open Mind* is an excellent resource for learning how to live in silence with God. If you like to use some form of the Jesus Prayer (see page 61) as a centering prayer, let it lead you to silence. If you can sit even five minutes a day in silence with God, you will notice your life changing. Gradually extend that to twenty minutes, and you'll see a new person staring back at you in the mirror.

5. Intercession

The fifth source of help for getting direction from God is the intercession of the saints, including the Blessed Virgin herself. Just as you may be asking Saint Anthony to help you in finding your lost keys or watch or glasses, so pray that Mary will intercede for you as you seek direction.

6. Spiritual Direction

If you want more help and guidance with your spiritual life, you might seek a spiritual director. This is usually a priest, monk, sister, or trained lay person who is especially gifted with wisdom and who will take your spiritual journey with you. One person may find that their pastor is the right spiritual director for them. Another may prefer to separate their personal spiritual direction from involvement in their faith community. Whatever his or her personal vocation, your director will give you suggestions about your reading, your prayers, and your Bible study, but will *not* be a psychotherapist; if you need help with problems in your daily life or marriage or career, see a counselor.

Listening to God

However you find guidance, *listen*! God speaks to us without ceasing, tenderly urging us to serve one another, to bring about the spread of the kingdom, and to show love to a broken world. Sometimes what God calls you to do is *nothing*. That's right, nothing. Perhaps God simply wants your company. There are days when God says, "Let's just be together a little while."

This is the time when you sit quietly in silent prayer, centering prayer, or meditation. If you've never tried it, sit down, take a deep breath, close your eyes, and just *be*. If you're a busy person, God may want you to relax in the divine or to delight in the Word, just as Mary of Bethany did when she sat at Christ's feet. Listen. The silence of God is not empty nor is it lonely. Wherever God is, there is more love than you may have imagined.

What about seeking specific guidance for a problem or a decision? You'll have to pray diligently, of course, and listen for God's answer. If you think you have an answer, confirm it with your spiritual director or a trusted Christian friend. If you still don't hear any guidance, you can propose one or two answers, believe that you'll know the will of God, and draw straws for the answer. Does that sound like a trivial idea? Well, it's the way eleven devout disciples used to choose Matthias as successor to Judas! (See Acts 1:23-26.)

Saint Ignatius of Loyola has left us another method for making decisions. First, believe that you will hear the will of God. Then fold a piece of paper and on the left side write all the pros, or *good* things about making the decision a particular way, and on the right side jot down all the reasons not to do it. Write honestly: don't add more weight to the side you think is right! After you've written all the things both for and against the decision, choose the one with the most items on it.

Author Mary Warren once weighed her life using this Ignatian method. Her husband had left her and her older children had moved far away, pursuing lifestyles that gave Mary great distress. She was having desperate money problems and her health was poor. But as she says in her book *Let the Earth Bring Forth*, she "realized how much of depression is linked with ingratitude." So on one half of a sheet of paper, she wrote down all the miserable things that had happened to her and on the other half, all the gifts that life had given her. She says, "The second list ended running right off the page. I'd included everything imaginable: daisies and bumblebees, homemade bread, the laughter of small children, clean sheets and hot baths, reading in bed at night, bonfires on the beach, snowflakes and minnows, shafts of sunlight, and the sound of rain."

living her words

1. The Jesus Prayer

This prayer—"Lord Jesus Christ, Son of God, have mercy on me, a sinner"—apparently rose out of the Russian Orthodox tradition. Many versions of *The Way of the Pilgrim* have been printed to explain the prayer and its history. Catholic bookstores usually carry a number of books or booklets about this prayer. It is one excellent way to become better able to listen to God. This week, choose one method of quiet prayer, either the Jesus prayer or centering prayer (see page 59). Set aside five to twenty minutes once or twice a day to practice your quiet prayer.

2. An Ignatian Method

You can use an Ignatian method to measure your progress in obeying God's commands. At the end of each day, jot down a list of your day's activities on the left side of a sheet of paper. You might start with

- went to work
- sold three new accounts
- picked up fast food for supper
- sorted recycling

Also write down your emotional and spiritual endeavors, whether you planned them or not:

- listened to Joanne talk about her drug-addicted son
- visited Mom at the nursing home
- played computer game with my daughter while we ate fast food

Then on the right side of the paper, jot the ways your activity revealed God's glory, or showed love, or increased someone's faith, just as the miracle at Cana increased the disciples' faith. Your attention to your daughter and listening to your friend's trouble weren't only acts of love, they were faithbuilders. This is what's called "lifestyle evangelism." Your recycling project showed respect for God's planet. If you were kind and patient with the fast-food server, and perhaps added a word of encouragement, you did God's work. Your visit to the nursing home was an act of love and obedience to the commandment to honor your father and mother.

How about your job? In the process of selling the three new accounts, were you able to bring some love into another person's life? Did you sell honestly? Or if you do some kind of labor, did you use your skills to the glory of God, offering your work up as service?

Sometimes what God tells you to do is something small. Instead of dispatching you to western Africa to work with the poor and HIV infected, God may send you to a four-year-old child who wants to understand about Noah and the ark. Instead of creating a great religious sculpture, God may ask you to plant daffodil bulbs on your window sill to brighten up the neighborhood. Instead of becoming a great teacher for Christ, maybe God wants you to compliment your market clerk on her new haircut as she scans your groceries. But whether the command is a large one, such as becoming a religious or getting married, or something as small as buying a package of sugarless gum for your godchild, *do* whatever God tells you.

The more you imitate Mary in doing whatever God wants you to do, the more ready you become for a life of real courage, a life of becoming what God wants you to *be*.

reflections

What was the most difficult thing God asked me to do today?
What person has God put in my life to test my willingness to live God's way?
What spirit does Mary put into my life?

CHAPTER NINE

day by day with mary

Devoting Yourself to Prayer

All these were constantly devoting themselves to prayer, together with…Mary the mother of Jesus

Acts 1:14

∞

God,
let me live with Mary,
and let me follow in her footsteps. Amen

Our Lord's Mother is an important figure in the history of Christian art. We've seen her portrayed in thousands of paintings, sculptures, and stained glass windows. When we seek a powerful symbol of grief, we find it in Michelangelo's exquisitely sorrowful *Pietà*. We love the rounded form of her veil in the myriad portrayals of Mother and Child. We stand in awe before the world's favorite Russian icon, *Our Lady of Vladimir*, by Anton Rublev. Perhaps no other person except our Lord himself has been so often painted or sculpted or gazed upon.

But Mary isn't just a lovely face on a Christmas card or in a marble carving. And she's certainly more than an archetype or religious symbol. Mary isn't a modern version of the goddess of pre-Christian religions. She's not only a representative of the feminine face of the Church. Mary is more than just an inspiring historical figure, more than just a saintly woman whose life we admire or try to emulate. She is also part of many daily lives right now, in present time. Those who pray regularly with Mary and the millions who daily recite the rosary aren't people who are just remembering a long-ago figure.

For them, Mary is here, now, today. These Christians are celebrating the life of a living woman with whom they have a relationship and pursue a dialogue. Through her they move closer to God. They will tell you she's active not only in heaven but in the world. Many persons—women in particular—tell about the presence of Mary when they needed help.

A woman in Phoenix, Arizona, says:

When our child died, I thought I would die, too. But suddenly, I knew a Presence in our home. Until then, I'd spent several days with frowsy hair, living in my bathrobe, weeping constantly. But when She came, I bathed and dressed up every day with the knowledge that Mary was telling me to look nice, to perfume myself, and be composed for the sake of others who needed me. I got through the funeral with her holding my hand, and she stayed for weeks afterward.

Another deeply religious woman in Portland, Oregon, was going through an unwanted divorce and a stressful job change. She reports that she looked over one night at the chair by her bed:

You know, *that* chair? The one that holds a week-old newspaper, three books, a box of tissues, maybe a dried-up peanut butter sandwich that you forgot to eat? One night I realized that Someone was waiting to sit in that chair! I didn't *see* Mary, but I knew she was there. I cleared off the chair, put the books on the bookshelf, and made a place in both my room and my heart for Mary. She stayed with me nearly a year, sitting in my bedroom chair as I woke up and fell asleep. Finally I had adjusted to my new job, the divorce was over, and I'd made peace with God about the things that had happened to me. Without her, I might *still* be angry with God.

And finally, a successful woman in Colorado writes:

My husband had been laid off at work, and his unemployment finally expired. We had to move 100 miles so he could take another job—one that paid half what he was used to. I had gone back to school and earned my teaching credentials, but the only job I found in the new city was clerking at a drugstore postal station. We were behind on everything—mortgage payments, car payments, doctor bills. The day after my oldest son was diagnosed as having severe attention deficit disorder, I went outside and found that both our cars had been repossessed. I walked the two miles to work, thinking I would go crazy. Someone loaned my husband a car and my mother came to help, but after she had to go back to work, Mary, my other Mother, came to stay with me until we got our lives sorted out. Without her, I might have given up; but with her, I was hopeful. I kept applying for teaching jobs until I got a good one. My husband was called back to his old job. We got our son into counseling and were able to send him to Catholic school.

These are only three in thousands of stories from men and women who experience Mary in their lives. Of course, she doesn't just come when we're miserable. Many people thank God for Mary when they get up in the morning and pray to her intermittently during the entire day.

Living with Mary

Life with Mary is many things, but it is first of all a life of prayer. Her very presence inspires prayer. According to the Acts of the Apostles, the first apostles met daily with her, "constantly devoting themselves to prayer" (Acts 1:14), and she was present with them in that upper room when the fire fell at Pentecost. Some very early paintings showing the coming of the Holy Spirit depict our Lord's Mother seated on a throne with tongues of fire leaping over her crowned head.

Today, all over the world, believers pray with Mary as the source of their devotion, emulating Mary's love for her son. Mary is often referred to as Mediatrix of All Graces. This title doesn't necessarily mean that all grace *must* be mediated through Mary, because that would negate the atoning work of Christ on the cross. It means that all graces, such as faith, hope, love, and forgiveness, *can* be mediated through her. Those who are reluctant, because they feel unworthy or too fearful, to directly approach the throne of God in prayer may find that Mary's intercession makes that throne more accessible. Praying with Mary means praying with someone who is in a perpetual state of grace and who rejoices in interceding for us.

Life with Mary isn't all joy, however; it can be a life of pain, for hers was. When Mary and Joseph presented the infant Jesus at the Temple in Jerusalem, Simeon thanked God for having seen the Messiah. Then Simeon blessed them and said to Mary, "This child is destined for the falling and the rising of many in Israel, and to be a sign that will be opposed so that the inner thoughts of many will be revealed—and a sword will pierce your own soul too" (Luke 2:34-35).

Surely a sword did pierce Mary's soul, nearly every day of her life. Her son never really belonged to her on earth, the way most children belong to their mothers. A chill must have penetrated Mary's spirit that day in Jerusalem when Jesus was twelve, because she saw there the beginning of the end. When he was grown, her son didn't settle down in the carpenter's shop and marry, giving Mary a loving daughter-in-law and a rich old age with grandchildren around her; instead, Jesus went off preaching, traveling the dusty roads with a ragtag group of followers. She watched the growing movement against Jesus and knew the chief priests were plotting against him. She watched the nails penetrate his wrists as he was crucified. She stood with John to watch her son die. And when the soldier's lance wounded Jesus' side, it stabbed Mary, too.

So although she cares for those in pain, Mary doesn't promise happiness or success. In fact, the Church teaches that pain is redemptive and that our goal should be heaven, not success on earth.

What Mary *can* do for anyone in pain is to fill them with hope and faith in Christ. Often they can eventually achieve that success themselves, as in the case of the woman from Colorado who finally got a good teaching job.

Life with Mary is ultimately a life of selflessness and devotion to God. Just as she was Israel's purest vessel for the Incarnation, so a strong

day by day with mary

relationship with her will purify *you* and help make you fit for the kingdom of heaven. I have a friend who says, "What with Jesus and Mary working on me all the time, I don't have a chance for any serious sin." Of course you will always have free will, and God allows you the freedom to sin. But as my friend says, with Jesus and Mary working on you and with the Holy Spirit working *in* you, your will to sin will diminish.

Think of Mary's life on earth: yes, a sword pierced her heart, but she who had willingly surrendered to God as a young girl continued to live for God. Her reward? The Church teaches us that the Blessed Virgin Mary is glorified in heaven more than any other earthly being. That's God's desire for you, too—that you also become a pure vessel for the love of Jesus Christ and rise to glory in heaven. Mary's daily ministry is to intercede for you.

Starting Your New Life

Just as you constantly welcome Jesus into your heart and mind, you can solicit Mary's presence by inviting her into your everyday life. Remember that Mary seeks to glorify her son, so each morning, say the Our Father and ask Jesus Christ to bless your day, sending his mother to be your companion.

Next you can use the prayers of Mary that you have explored in this book. You might want to use the prayer of awe and wonder on Monday, the prayer of assent on Tuesday, and so on. On Sunday you'll join Mary in the prayers at Mass. Then you can start the cycle again, devoting yourself constantly to prayer in the presence of our Lord's Mother, just as the apostles did in Acts 1:14: "[They] were constantly devoting themselves to prayer, together with…Mary the mother of Jesus."

Try to write something about Mary in your journal every day, even if it's just *one sentence* at bedtime or on rising; for example, you can write a prayer—"Dear Mother Mary, pray with me today as I ask for a raise at work"—or an idea—"Mary was not only a mother but also a daughter. I want to be the kind of daughter she was to Saint Anne." In the next chapter, we'll take a deeper look at prayer practices and journal techniques.

The Priesthood of Mary

Mary has special offices to perform for us: she is a link to God's Incarnation, and she prays with us when we ask her. She invites us to purity and selflessness, gently urging us toward the salvation of Jesus, toward a life in grace.

I was privileged one day to find on the World Wide Web a short homily called "The Priesthood of Mary," signed by a Dominican nun who identifies herself only as Sister Monica. Part of this short message said:

> This is the priesthood of Mary; the priesthood of holiness. It is a call to separateness and isolation. An isolation that makes me available to others, able to hold others as Mary holds the helpless baby Jesus, because I have put aside the distractions that hinder the union of love between persons in union with God. I must not intrude but must learn to live in the mystery and paradox of alone together and together alone.

living her words

1. Review

Re-read your journal entries about the three Bible passages that you chose to reflect on at the end of the first chapter. How has your point of view changed since you read those Scriptures and meditated upon them? Would you choose the same ones today? In what ways have *you* changed since you made those entries?

2. Meditate

Ponder those same three Bible events in a prayerful state, and again see yourself present in them. This time, listen closely to what both Mary and your own heart are saying. Allow yourself to take a prominent part in the events: for instance, if you accompany Mary and Joseph on the flight to Egypt, imagine yourself the caravan leader, or a nurse who helps care for the infant Jesus. Pay attention to Mary's personality: how does she treat Joseph and their fellow travelers? How does she feel about going to Egypt, and does she think Joseph is correct in insisting that they go? Is she really afraid of Herod, or does she remember the prophecies of Gabriel and Simeon and know that her child is protected?

3. Journal a Description

Write a description of Mary. Take your time in this journaling; use several sessions to finish it if necessary. Write down what you think she looked like, how she *really* dressed (not just the traditional blue veil), her hair and eye color, her size, and how she walked. Then write what you think her personality was like before the Resurrection of Jesus and before she was elevated to her present heavenly status.

4. Journal Your Changes

Write a brief description in your journal about how living with Mary has changed you, your lifestyle, your relationships, or even your personality.

reflections

How will daily life with Mary change me?
How has God given me more life as I have explored praying with Mary?
Am I afraid of these changes?

CHAPTER TEN

transformation

Becoming the Pure Vessel

Do not be conformed to this world, but be transformed by the renewing of your minds, so that you may discern what is the will of God—what is good and acceptable and perfect.

Romans 12:2

O God,
transform me
that I might become worthy of Christ.
Let me, like Mary,
be pure and full of your grace;
and let me seek your face
through my prayer and study. Amen

There's a story that emerges in newspapers, magazines, and sermons every year around Christmas. The story is ostensibly about a businessman, his wife, his daughter, and a flock of birds, but the story is really an investigation of Christ's Incarnation.

That man, who lived on a modest estate in the Northeast, was kind to his family, easygoing and fair with his employees, and generous in charitable giving. His only problem was that he didn't believe in God. His wife and daughter were faithful churchgoers, and he *wanted* to believe, but his rational mind said that if there was a God who created the universe, that God simply wouldn't become a man to redeem humanity.

"Why do we need redeeming?" he always asked when he played golf with the local priest. "I can't believe we do, or that any God would condescend to do it instead of showing us how to redeem ourselves."

His wife and daughter left one cold, snowy Christmas Eve for Midnight Mass, and although he didn't accompany them, he waited up, keeping the fire going because he was a loving husband and father. He sat in his easy chair and read the *Wall Street Journal* from cover to cover. Then he went to the closet and took down the special Christmas surprises he'd bought for his wife and daughter. By then it was after eleven o'clock, and the temperature had dipped to zero. Suddenly he heard *thump! thump!* in the living room. He discovered that some small birds were flying into the big picture window, trying to get to light and warmth. Two were lying dead in the snow.

He felt so sorry for the birds he almost wept. He bundled up and went out to the barn, turning on the light and leaving the door open so the birds could get in; but they kept throwing themselves against the glass. He tried scattering grain from the house to the barn, hoping they'd follow the food trail. Still the birds hurt themselves, trying to get into the house and ignoring his efforts to help them.

Finally he stood in the snow, frustrated, and said to himself, "The only way I could help these poor creatures would be to become a bird myself, and show them the way."

At that moment, he heard the church bells ring: it was midnight and the beginning of Christmas, the festival of the Incarnation. He fell to his knees in the snow and prayed, saying, "O God, I understand, and I believe."

God *did* come as Jesus, to show the way to us poor, sinful "birds." All other efforts—the law, the leaders of Israel, the words of the prophets—had failed. The only way human beings would get on the path to warmth and safety was for God to become human. And God didn't just *appear* to be human or just manifest as a full-grown human being. He had to have real human experiences. To be not only truly God but also truly human, God the Son had to be born of a woman.

Which leads us to two very important questions: What kind of woman did God choose? And how do we follow in her footsteps?

God's View of Mary

The answers may be found in the biblical words of the Hail Mary. No wonder Catholics love the rosary, for in it, they get to affirm who Mary is.

Gabriel saluted Mary as a woman "full of grace." He didn't mean she was pretty, well-liked, or clever at weaving or cooking (whether she was or not). He meant she was a pure vessel, full of the grace of God, prayerful and loving. Only a woman of unsurpassed virtue was worthy to rear Jesus, the Incarnate God.

Grace comes from a word meaning "gift," and it's a concept that is developed by New Testament writers: "The law indeed was given through Moses; grace and truth came through Jesus Christ" (John 1:17). God's coming to earth in the person of Jesus was the ultimate grace. So when Gabriel acknowledged that Mary was full of grace, he recognized that God had already prepared her to be Christ's mother. And just as God filled Mary with grace, the gifts you need from God are reserved for you.

"The Lord is with you," Gabriel continued, telling her—and us—what kind favor God had bestowed upon this young Galilean woman. Notice the angel doesn't say "The Lord loves you" or "God sends you blessing." Gabriel says that God is already *with* her. That means Mary had already, even as a girl in her teens, invited God to live in her heart. When you were baptized, you or your sponsors asked God to enter your life forever, and the Lord is with you!

The prayer continues with Elizabeth's words: "Blessed are you among women." *Blessed* doesn't mean *lucky*; when people *bless* the Lord, they're praising and thanking God. When she pronounced that Mary was blessed, Saint Elizabeth was affirming Mary's holiness—in fact, everyone who knew Mary must have recognized the perfection of her spirit, even before the events in Bethlehem. A *blessed* person is one who shines with the Spirit, and when you seek holiness, you, too, have that inner glow that tells people you're blessed.

Transformed by the Renewal of your Minds

God calls all men and women, not to be the mother of Jesus Christ, because the Incarnation was a once-for-all-time event, but to be transformed. It's our privilege to become the sign of God's love and mercy in a broken world, showing by our transformed lives that the kingdom of God is among us.

Mary also calls us to transformation: in February 1996, the young people who hear her message at Medjugorje reported that she said, "This is the most important message that I have given you here. I invite you, little children, to live the messages that I have given you over these years. This time is a time of grace, especially now when *the Church also is inviting you to prayer and conversion.*"

What Is Conversion?

Conversion is change, and the world is full of God's changes. Seeds fall into the soil and split open so that the corn or dahlia or redwood essences deep within them can burst forth. The seed disappears so that it can become not a hard little kernel, but a glorious plant. A caterpillar "dies" in its cottony cocoon so it can emerge as a beautiful butterfly; the butterfly was present in the caterpillar all along.

Sea water becomes vapor, and then clouds, and then falls as rain on farms and forests. These changes take time, but they're ordained from the beginning. In the same way, the perfect man or woman that God sees in you has existed from your beginning, and through living a holy life, you can begin to let that *real* person shine forth.

Sometimes God makes rapid conversions. When Jesus converted water to wine, the very essence of the water had to be changed. If that water had fallen as rain onto the soil of a vineyard and had nourished the plants, it would have eventually become the juice that forms inside the skins of grapes; then, to become not just grape juice but wine, it would have had to undergo the fermentation process. Jesus probably let this entire process happen in a few seconds, bypassing the limitations of time. What the water had once been no longer existed.

Whether you change slowly like the redwood seed or whether you experience a remarkable conversion, once you begin letting God change you, your old nature is converted and finally no longer exists. Undoubtedly, that process would have felt scary if you were a seed or a caterpillar or a molecule of water. So you may have the sensation that you're dying, that you're losing yourself. Jesus has spoken to this sensation: "Very truly, I tell you, unless a grain of wheat falls into the earth and dies, it remains just a single grain; but if it dies, it bears much fruit" (John 12:24). He went on to say that the person who clings to this life will die, but the one who discards this existence will reap eternal life.

In *Mere Christianity*, C.S. Lewis talks about toy soldiers. Most children like to imagine that their toy could come to life. But the toy might be reluctant: "He is not interested in flesh; all he sees is that the tin is being spoilt. He will do everything he can to prevent you."

We humans also try to prevent our being changed not from tin to flesh but from mortal to immortal. The world has only seen one real Man, who was also the Son of God. Only one human being ever allowed God to complete the transformation process completely through life, death, and resurrection. Lewis says, "One tin soldier—real tin, just like the rest—had come fully and splendidly alive."

Through that life we too can have immortality. But we need to ask for it or rather say to God, *Yes, transform me; make me into a real man or woman.*

Supporting Your Conversion

The Bible, Mary, and the Church invite you to prayer and to conversion, as evidenced by the Medjugorje message. Conversion means a new way of life. The Holy Spirit starts the change and you support it—devotion to the Mass, love for God, a sturdy relationship with Mary, constant prayer, meditation, intimate familiarity with the Scriptures, daily invocation of the Holy Spirit, and a conscious acceptance of Christ's sacrifice for your personal redemption.

You can tell when conversion takes place, because you have *more* life, not less. Your enjoyment of the created universe will probably increase, and you'll still work in your garden or keep books or program computers (unless God calls you to some new ministry); but life will be different. The more you pray, the more you study the Bible, the more compassion and gentleness you will build within yourself. The "tin" of your life may be ruined, and you may lose your enjoyment of some worldly pursuits, but you will become a person others call "blessed," a man or woman of God.

Remember that before the universe was formed, God knew you by name and loved you. Now God asks that you return that love and intimacy by becoming what Mary is—the pure receptacle of the Spirit.

living her words

1. Design Your Transformation

Decide who you want to become, and record this in your journal. Write down the attributes you would like to present to the world, such as mercy, gentleness, love, faith, holiness, or whatever other qualities God calls you to show. Remember as you make this plan that you are the sign of God's love for a sad and suffering world.

2. Pray

Ask God to show you what you need to do to achieve this transformation. Do you need to study the Bible more, give more time to charity, pray with greater fervor, or mortify some habits like overeating? As you begin to receive answers to this prayer, through private revelation or in the words of other people, write them in your journal. Test these answers to see if they really aid your conversion.

3. Get a Partner

Ask Mary to be your companion in this venture. Ask her to bless your desire to be transformed and to intercede for you.

4. Chart Success—Yours and God's

When you notice that you react with gentleness instead of a hot temper, when you show someone more kindness than you thought you were capable of, write down the dates when you first notice these changes. Each time you achieve one of the qualities you listed in your transformation plan, record it—and thank God for filling you with this grace.

reflections

In what ways was I transformed today?
What life-giving gifts has God given me through grace?
How will my transformation make me more like Mary?

using the way of mary

for Retreats and Small-Group Study

Retreats and Shorter Gatherings

For a weekend retreat or a quiet day, use some or all of the subjects in this book. If possible, provide every retreatant with a copy to take home for further study and activity.

Start the day with prayer, including the Hail Mary (or the rosary, if time permits).

Bring the retreatants together ten times, if possible and if you plan to use all the chapters. Use each chapter subject as a fifteen-minute meditation. Before you begin each session, light a candle, read the prayer at the beginning of the chapter, then describe the setting of the story and read the Bible passage. If you have pictures or other suitable graphics to accompany some of the Bible events, you might display them on an easel.

Cover the basic material as briefly as necessary. For example, for chapter 1, recount the times Mary appears in Scripture, pointing out the only four scenes in which she speaks. Wherever possible, make these scenes live by fleshing out the characters involved in each scene. As you proceed through each subject, make sure the retreatants grasp the words of Mary as *prayers* they can use in their own lives.

In looking at Bible events, present Mary as a real woman, not as the Queen of Heaven. In the Bible story she is first a young Galilean girl, later a worried mother, and finally the mother of the adult Jesus. Making her a flesh-and-blood woman will help retreatants identify with her and finally to pray *with* her in her own words.

If this is not a silent event, allow questions and answers, then use some of the reflection material at the end of each chapter for discussion. Optimally, the group will break into pairs or triads to answer one or more questions or to discuss ways they would like to pursue enriching ther lives in Mary. At the end of each session, hand each person the words of that chapter's prayer and the *reflection* questions, then send the retreatants in silence to their rooms or let them find solitary, silent places for meditation outdoors.

At the end of the retreat, encourage the retreatants to share their experience of living and praying with Mary. Finish with the Eucharist, allowing each retreatant to write a promise to Mary on a piece of paper and place it in a container as a gift to her. Burn these promises during the preparation of gifts so that the retreatants know their offering is a private one.

Using *The Way of Mary* for Group Study

You can use this book for either a ten- to twelve-week program or a once-a-month group. An ideal meeting would include a brief liturgy, rosary, or prayer time; presentation of the material; discussion; related activity; and fellowship. This will probably take between ninety minutes and two hours. Following is a program design for a twelve-week program, including an introductory session and a debriefing or summing-up session at the end.

Session 1
Getting Started

Open this (and every) meeting by lighting a candle and saying the Our Father and the Hail Mary. Introduce *The Way of Mary* and give each participant a copy of the book to keep. Encourage the participants to mark and underline in their copies. Also, hand out notebooks or small bound books to use as journals through the study. Talk briefly about the spiritual and psychological value of journaling.

Next, begin to create community. Let participants introduce themselves and tell in one or two sentences what they hope to gain from the program. As they name these goals, write them on newsprint, and save this list for the last session.

Ask each person to choose a prayer partner for this study (or assign partners). These partners will pray for each other daily, and wherever possible, keep in touch by phone weekly.

Invite discussion about Mary. Who is she? Why was she chosen to be the mother of Christ? What traditions do the participants love most about Mary? What kind of personality do they think she had on earth? What is her relationship to the world? In this discussion, *everyone is right.* Don't teach doctrine; allow participants to express themselves in safety.

Discuss the Bible, and make sure each person has one at home (or provide inexpensive paperback New Testaments). Invite them to always bring to the meeting Bibles they can mark in, their copy of *The Way of Mary*, and their journals. Invite remarks about Bible reading and what the Church teaches about it.

Explain that they will be using the biblical words of Mary as *prayers*, not just as study resources. Remind them that praying the Scriptures is a form of prayer and meditation recognized by the Church. Invite discussion about praying the words of Mary.

Now ask the participants to keep silence for five minutes, reflecting on Mary and the group. Tell them that when they are finished with their reflection, they should date a journal page and write a few sentences about Mary and their relationship to her, whatever that may be.

Assign the reading for the next week, which includes the brief introduction and chapter 1, "The Virgin Mary: What the Bible Record Shows." Point out the section called "Living Her Words" at the end of each chapter, and suggest that they will be doing some of these activities together.

At the end of this session, say a brief prayer of closing, put out the candle, and provide simple refreshments, such as cookies and instant coffee or tea. Encourage the participants to get to know one another better during this time.

Session 2
The Virgin Mary:
What the Bible Record Shows

After opening prayers, read the passage from the First Letter of Peter (1:3) and the brief prayer that begin chapter 1. Briefly describe each appearance of Mary in the Bible, including the scenes in which her words are recorded. If you have pictures, icons, or other aids to learning and devotion, display them on easels. Encourage class members to place themselves in the Bible scenes as they listen to your summary.

Wherever possible, make these scenes live by fleshing out the characters involved in each scene. As you proceed through each subject, make sure the retreatants grasp the words of Mary as *prayers* they can use in their own lives.

In looking at Bible events, present Mary as a real woman, not as the Queen of Heaven. In the Bible story she is first a young Galilean girl, later a worried mother, and finally the mother of the adult Jesus. Making her a flesh-and-blood woman will help participants identify with her and finally to pray *with* her in her own words.

Invite discussion about these Bible appearances. Which are the most popular? Which the least? At which one of these events would the participants most like to be?

Ask each person to write down the three Bible passages they've chosen for meditation that week from the reflection pages. Then divide into prayer-partner groups, and discuss those Bible events. Why did they choose them? How will meditating on them change their lives?

After discussion, call for a few minutes of silent meditation, followed by the journaling assignment at the end of chapter 1. Before ending with prayer and fellowship, ask each person to *write* the questions from the chapter's "Reflections" section (page 6) in their journal and to use them every night that week. Then make the next week's reading assignment—chapter 2.

Session 3
How Can This Be?
The Prayer of Awe and Wonder

Use the usual pattern for prayers, and read the Bible passage. Try to display several pictures or icons of the Annunciation. In this week's discussion, ask each participant to name something that fills him or her with wonder, and to share with the group what that reaction feels like. Find out how many already tried using the words as prayers during the past week.

In the prayer-partner discussion, ask the partners to pray silently for each other for a full minute before talking. Then ask partners to talk about the Annunciation and the prayer of awe and wonder, using the questions in the first part of "Living Her Words" on page 13—"Look at Mary." After a few minutes of silence, ask participants to begin the journaling assignment in the book if they have time and to complete it during the week. Remind them to copy the chapter 2 reflection questions (page 14) into their journals for meditation each night.

Close this session by saying together Mary's words, "How can this be?" as a parting prayer. Before fellowship, remind the group of the next week's reading assignment.

Session 4
According to Your Word:
The Prayer of Assent to God

After praying together and then reading the chapter's gospel passage, discuss Mary's assent to God. Ask participants to describe a world in which Mary had said "No." Would Christ have been born anyway? If he hadn't been born, what would life have become?

Ask prayer partners to pray in silence for each other, then talk to each other about the times they've said *either* "yes" or "no" to God. Invite them to discuss their feelings about some or all of the words in the "Living Her Words" section, page 21—(God's will, Christ in me, trust, goodness, willingness, yes)—then to talk about the qualities displayed when Christ is born within their personalities.

Give each person a small stone to place in the bedroom or on a desk. Invite them to let the rock teach them obedience through their contemplating the ways a rock is obedient to God.

Ask participants to write in their journals a sentence or two about the value of assent to God. Then ask them to write down Mary's words of assent to use as a breath prayer or centering prayer for the week. Before prayers and fellowship, assign the next week's chapter and ask the class members to write their reflection questions for meditation each night. Close by saying together, "Let it be done to me according to your word."

Session 5
My Soul Magnifies the Lord:
The Prayer of Perfect Praise

If possible, begin this session by singing (or playing a recording of) "Jerusalem, My Happy Home." After prayers, read the Magnificat aloud *in unison*, using the version at the top of the chapter so that all will recite the same version.

Discuss the ways God works in this world, and the ways we must serve one another to make the Magnificat a reality, including filling the hungry with good things and exalting the lowly. Talk about the ways Christ has changed the lives of women from Bible times, especially in America.

Ask prayer partners to spend their discussion magnifying the Lord, discussing the ways in which a loving God has blessed creation and their own lives.

This week's assignment is different: ask the class members to use the reflection questions every night (page 31), to say the Magnificat as a personal prayer every day this week, and to end it by following the journal instructions on page 30. Close by saying the Magnificat together (page 30).

Session 6
Why Have You Treated Me This Way?
The Prayer of Intimate Confrontation

After the gospel reading and prayers, ask people to spend about two minutes remembering times in their lives when they felt angry at God. Ask them to reflect on this question: Do you feel, deep down, that you're not supposed to express anger at God? If so, why? If not, why not? After a minute or two, ask people to spend about five minutes quietly writing down those memories in their journals and beginning to answer the questions they've just reflected on. Whatever they are unable to complete should be finished at home.

Discuss the ways in which intimacy is enhanced by honesty and whether or not Mary was angry at her son for his disappearance. Was her reaction to him mild under the circumstances or harsh? Why do they think the Bible records no words from Joseph when he and Mary found Jesus?

Read Job 21 aloud to the class. How do they think Job felt about God? Point out that Job suggests all through this book that God allows chaos to break through, and that God is, though powerful, not necessarily *good*.

Ask prayer partners to pray in silence and then to discuss the times when they felt angry at God or times when they believe that God let them down. Encourage them to pray for each other.

Read the self-test questions from "Living Her Words", page 38, asking participants to write down their answers in their journals and then score themselves according to the book. Ask them to write a few sentences about anger at God.

Before prayers and fellowship, assign chapter 6 for reading that week and remind them to write the chapter 5 reflection questions into their journals. Close by saying together, "God, why have you treated me this way?"

Session 7
I Have Been Searching for You Anxiously:
The Prayer of Longing

If possible, open this session by singing or playing a recording of "Humbly I Adore Thee" (in Latin, "Adoro Te Devote"). Then after the gospel reading, ask someone to read aloud Psalm 42.

Ask class members to discuss times in their lives when someone important to them was absent by death, divorce, war, or other necessity. How long did it take to get used to their absence (if ever)? How did these class members express their grief and longing at the time? What would they have done to have the person return to their lives? Did they *really* want God as badly as they wanted that person?

Be prepared to discuss Bible characters, saints, and other religious figures who have expressed longing for God: David, Saint Thomas Aquinas, Saint Teresa of Avila, Julian of Norwich, or other historical figures. How did they deal with their hunger and thirst for God?

Take a few minutes of silence for the class to meditate on how using Mary's prayer of longing will bring them closer to God.

Ask prayer partners to make lists together of ways they can seek God, for example, in the Mass, in the Bible, or in nature. Encourage each participant to share with their partner some ways they have unexpectedly experienced the presence of God.

Before prayers and fellowship, assign the chapter 6 reflection questions and chapter 7 for reading. Close by saying together, "Jesus, I have been searching for you with great anxiety."

Session 8
They Have No Wine:
The Prayer of Intercession

Let the participants sit at a beautifully set table, with wine glasses, flowers, and candles, as if it were a wedding reception. Try to display some wedding pictures—photographs or clips from magazines—that show weddings and wedding receptions. If possible, display some pictures of a Jewish wedding, including the canopy and the breaking of the wine glass.

Pour wine (or fruit juice) into *some* of the glasses, letting some people go without. Explain that for everyone to have refreshments, those who have some can choose to share what they have, go out and buy more wine, or ask the "wine steward" for more. If the stores are closed and sharing will mean that nobody gets enough, suggest that they bow their heads and ask Jesus Christ to furnish more wine. Sit in silence for three full minutes; then let someone fill all the glasses.

Discuss what is most lacking in your community. This might include low-income housing, women's safety, money for schools, peace between gangs, a bike path, or good city officials. Now pass out newspaper clippings about someone's homelessness, illness, crime, war, or other problem. Furnish glue sticks so class members can choose three clippings and paste these clippings in their journals. Beneath each clipping, they should write, "They have no _____ (home, health, food, peace, safety, child, or whatever the particular need is)."

Prayer partners can now pray together for the people in these clippings and commit to praying all week for them.

Assign the chapter 7 reflection questions and chapter 8 reading for next week. Since fellowship started at the beginning of this session, it can continue after prayers. Close with the prayer, "God, the people have no more wine."

Session 9
Do Whatever He Tells You:
Finding Your Rule of Life

After opening prayers and the reading of the gospel, ask two questions: first, "Why did Mary persist, after Jesus first rejected her plea?" and then, "Why did Jesus perform this miracle?" *Let all answers be right,* as an experiment in shared hermeneutics.

Then discuss rules of life, including those in monasteries, such as the Benedictine or Augustinian. Ask the participants to talk about why people seek rules and how Mary's rule is both narrow and very liberal.

Finally, discuss how to know what God is calling you to do: does each person's rule include asking God what to buy in the grocery store, or does it apply only to big callings, such as religious vocation or marriage?

Prayer partners should now help each other follow the Ignatian exercise at the end of chapter 8. Don't rush this process; before fellowship, finish with prayers, a reminder to journal the reflection questions, and assignment of chapter 9 for next week. Close by saying *to one another,* "Do whatever he tells you."

Session 10
Day by Day with Mary
Devoting Yourself to Prayer

Display as many pictures of Mary as you can find, for example, photos of statues including the Michelangelo *Pietà*, Christmas cards with Madonnas, and holy cards portraying the Blessed Virgin. If you can find enough holy cards, give one to each participant.

After opening prayers, ask the participants to discuss the Bible passages they chose in session 2 and how they have changed in their attitude toward Mary since writing those down. If they were to choose today, would they select the same events or different ones? Why?

Discuss the personality Mary shows the world *in Scripture* (not through apparitions or other messages). Ask class members to break into prayer partner groups, where they will discuss two of those Bible stories in which Mary's words are not recorded. Encourage them to talk to each other about what Mary and their own hearts are saying. Ask them to place themselves *prominently* in the scene. How does Mary feel, and what are her thoughts during these events? How does she relate to her husband and son?

End the session with plenty of time to start journaling the description of Mary, number 3 of "Living Her Words" for chapter 9, page 69. Remind participants to journal their chapter 9 reflection questions during the week and read chapter 10. Close by saying together, "Mother Mary, let me follow in your footsteps."

Session 11
Transformation:
Becoming the Pure Vessel

Open the session by lighting a candle and a stick of incense and playing a tape of a hymn or meditative music. Discuss transformation and conversion. The man in the snow was *converted*; the water at Cana was *transformed*. How are these the same? How are they different?

What did Saint Paul mean when he said, "Do not be conformed to this world, but be transformed by the renewing of your minds, so that you may discern what is the will of God—what is good and acceptable and perfect" (Romans 12:2). What is the renewing of minds?

In what ways does the world need to be transformed? We use the phrase "in a perfect world." What would go on in a perfect world of God's design?

Read the following passage from Revelation 21:1-4:

> Then I saw a new heaven and a new earth; for the first heaven
> and the first earth had passed away, and the sea was no more.
> And I saw the holy city, the new Jerusalem, coming down out
> of heaven from God, prepared as a bride adorned for her hus-
> band. And I heard a loud voice from the throne saying,
>
> > "See, the home of God is among mortals.
> > He will dwell with them as their God;
> > they will be his peoples,
> > and God himself will be with them;
> > he will wipe every tear from their eyes.
> > Death will be no more;
> > mourning and crying and pain will be no more,
> > for the first things have passed away."

Ask the participants to meditate silently on this passage for three or
four minutes, then to take turns saying out loud (without explanation) the
word or phrase that caught their attention.

Let prayer partners help each other begin designing their transformation, writing this design in their journals as instructed in "Living Her Words"
for chapter 10 on page 76. At closing, assign the reflection questions and
pray together the prayer at the beginning of that chapter: O God, transform me that I might become worthy of Christ. Let me, like Mary, be pure
and full of your grace; and let me seek your face through my prayer and
study. Amen.

Session 12
Summing Up

If this group will not be continuing to meet together, this should be an
informal session to break community by saying goodbye to each other.
Whether the group is ending or continuing, participants (including the
leader) should debrief or sum up what they have learned and experienced.
Use the list that the group generated at the first session to remind people
where they began and what their goals were. If possible, end this session
with a Eucharist followed by a festive supper or major snack.

about the author

K risten Johnson Ingram is the author of nine other books, including *Blessing Your Enemies, Forgiving Your Friends* (Liguori Publications, 1993), twelve booklets, and more than a thousand magazine and newspaper articles, as well as short fiction and poetry. Besides leading retreats and conferences, Kristen is a licensed preacher and Eucharistic Minister in the Episcopal Church and is recognized as a spiritual director in her diocese. She is the mother of three grown children and has five grandsons. Her mystery novel, *Angel in the Senate*, will be published in 1998. She works and lives with her husband Ron in a house at the edge of the woods in Springfield, Oregon.

MORNING STAR
Christ's Mother and Ours
Oscar Lukefahr, C.M.
An explanation of Mary's special place in God's plan—based on Scripture and Church teachings, art and architecture, song and sacramentals, devotion and apparitions. Indexed. **$7.95**
*Companion workbook also available...***$2.95**

OUR LADY OF THE JOURNEY NOTE CARDS
This beautiful illustration of the pregnant Madonna has brought inspiration and joy to many. Now her image has been captured on these special note cards! An original prayer by Francine O'Connor to Our Lady of the Journey is printed on the inside, with the right side blank for your own personal message. Box of 10 cards with 10 envelopes. **$10.95**

THE STORY OF
OUR MOTHER OF PERPETUAL HELP
Redemptorist Pastoral Communications
■**Video** This video explores the legacy of one of the Church's most revered icons—explaining the symbolism, the style, the message, and the story behind the famous picture. It includes personal memories of the sacred icon from Pope John Paul II during a visit to the actual shrine in Rome. 30 minutes, VHS. **$19.95**

QUEEN OF PEACE
Stained Glass Screen Saver
Queen of Peace is a collection of images taken from traditional and contemporary stained glass windows featuring Mary. These are photographs of windows found in churches all over the United States and Canada! Each image was chosen for its attention to detail, color, clarity, and theme. **$19.95**
System Requirements:
• IBM PC or compatible • Windows 3.1 or later • 3.5" high density drive • 6MB hard drive space • VGA monitor set at 256 colors